'As with Larkin, I prefer Priestley grumbling to most other writers enthusing.' – Alan Bennett

J. B. Priestley (1894–1984) was born in Yorkshire and fought in the Great War before going to Trinity Hall, Cambridge. He was a novelist, playwright, prolific essayist, broadcaster, scriptwriter, social commentator and man of letters. His twenty-eight short 'Postscripts', broadcast during the war, were considered more influential than Churchill's. Priestley's best-known play, *An Inspector Calls*, continues to be staged all over the world.

Valerie Grove has been a journalist for fifty years, writin recently about Priestley in the *New Statesman* (2014) ar the *Guardian Review* (2015). She read English at Girt College, Cambridge and has been on the staff of the *Even Standard*, *The Sunday Times* and *The Times*, as an intervie reviewer and columnist. Her books include biographi Dodie Smith, Laurie Lee, John Mortimer and Kaye V She is a Tynesider by origin – but has lived in London adolescence and has four children.

GRUMBLING AT LARGE

–

Selected Essays of J. B. Priestley

–

with an introduction by

Valerie Grove

nh Notting Hill Editions

Published in 2016
by Notting Hill Editions Ltd
Widworthy Barton Honiton Devon EX14 9JS

Designed by FLOK Design, Berlin, Germany
Typeset by CB editions, London

Printed and bound by Memminger MedienCentrum, Memmingen, Germany

The essays in this book have been reproduced by kind permission of the
J. B. Priestley Estate: 'On Beginning', 'A Coincidence' and 'All About
Ourselves' from *I For One*, 1923; 'Having Covered the Card Table' from
Open House, 1927; 'First Snow' from *Apes and Angels*, 1928; 'Carless
at Last' and 'My Forchern' from *The Balconinny*, 1929; 'Dissolution in
Haymarket', 'On the Moors', 'Strange Encounter' and 'Different Inside'
from *Self-Selected Essays*, 1932; 'The Reunion Battalion Dinner' from
English Journey, 1934; 'Wednesday 5 June 1940' and 'Sunday 9 June
1940' from *Postscripts*, 1940; 'Eros and Logos', 'On Education', 'Another
Revolution' and 'Televiewing' from *Thoughts in the Wilderness*, 1957;
'Women Don't Run the Country' from the *Saturday Evening Post*, 1964;
'The Moments', 'Tobacco', and 'Giving Up Conferences' from *Moments and
Other Pieces*, 1966; 'Old Age', 'Happiness' and 'On Hating Airports' from
Instead of the Trees, 1977; 'Critique of 1972' from *Priestley's Wars*, 2008.

Frontispiece image: J. B. Priestley Archive, Special Collections, University
of Bradford

A CIP record for this book is available from the British Library

ISBN 978-1-910749-18-0

www.nottinghilleditions.com

Contents

Much of my writing, I have no doubt, consists of adverse criticism of this life, and so is a sort of grumbling at large. There is some self-indulgence here, I will grant you, but there is also a speck or two of something better. For I have always felt that a writer, if only to justify some of his privileges, should speak for those who cannot easily speak for themselves.

J. B. Priestley, 'Preface, or The Grumbler's Apology', 1949

Valerie Grove

– Introduction –

In a cloud of pipe smoke, J. B. Priestley told his son Tom: 'I always knew what I was going to do with myself, and I've never regretted making writing my profession.' After another puff, he added, 'I'm more a writer than a human being, I think.' This strikingly self-aware declaration was made in front of Tom's camera, during what was planned as an affectionate television portrait of his father for his 90th birthday. But since JBP died at 89, the film went out on his death, in 1984.

The programme showed viewers the familiar image of John Boynton Priestley, OM, popularly known as Jack, in the library of Kissing Tree House near Stratford-upon-Avon, the splendid Georgian manor where he spent his last twenty-five years with his third wife, Jacquetta Hawkes. Here was that scowly, jowly face, usually photographed under a black hat. 'A stocky figure in a plum-coloured velvet jacket and a mask of melancholy resignation', as one biographer put it. Priestley agreed. Coming from the West Riding of Yorkshire, which 'favours the grumbler', he wrote, 'I have always been a grumbler. I was designed for the part, for I have a sagging face, a weighty underlip, what I am told is a "saurian eye" and a rumbling but resonant voice from which it is difficult to escape. Money could not buy a better grumbling outfit.' This is from 'The Grumbler's Apology', the opening essay in a 1949 volume called *Delight*, about the variety of things – 114 in number, varying from dancing to making stew – that bring him joy.

Readers of Priestley's novels love his characters, brought to life via their distinctive voices, including Dickensian quirks that make even villains appealing. Playgoers admire Priestley's ingenious plots, generally likeable dramatis personae, strong messages. But with a handful of notable exceptions, his essays have tended to be more ephemeral. The essay defies classification, but a habitual essayist must have a vigorously singular voice – it came naturally to Priestley – to be permitted to say, as Hazlitt put it, 'whatever passed through his mind'. Priestley's output was prolific, even in his twenties. The essays translated into 15-minute broadcasts during World War II, when Priestley's *Postscripts* were regarded as more powerful than Churchill's broadcasts, and just as inspiring. In the 1950s, the pieces he wrote for Kingsley Martin at the *New Statesman* began to influence public opinion, especially his 1957 piece on why Britain should ban the bomb. He is still regarded as a founding voice of CND.

Readers of the early essays in this collection will discover a younger Jack Priestley, not yet famous or polemical, an amiable, inquisitive fellow, curious about everything, prone to find magic in unexpected things. The display and artifice of his youthful essays places them in the Victorian tradition, animated by a talent to amuse.

J. B. Priestley's antecedents were proletarian – one grandfather worked at the mill, his grandmother's family were silk weavers – but his father, Jonathan, had been sent to teacher training college. Jonathan Priestley 'was the man Socialists have in mind when they talk about Socialism,' Jack wrote, 'but never joined the Labour Party.' (Nor did Jack.) Priestley senior rose to be headmaster of an elementary school, the first in the country to provide meals for its pupils. Jack describes Bradford as 'a city entirely without charm . . . but it has the good fortune to be on the edge of some of the most enchanting country in England.' Enriched by the wool trade, the Bradford of his youth possessed all the progressive and cultural hallmarks of a flourishing Victorian city: two theatres, a permanent orchestra, two choral societies, two music-halls, three daily newspapers and well-stocked libraries. Having left school at sixteen, Jack was aware of this luck: 'It was not that I went to the right sort of school, but that I was living in the right sort of town.' Its very atmosphere encouraged intellectual growth. And with his articles and reviews for a local paper Jack Priestley could learn his craft, writing in his bedroom with its fierce little gas fire 'that could not begin to warm the room without grilling your shins'. His day-job was as a clerk with Messrs Helm & Company in Swan Arcade, wool purveyors, where 'I was allowed to be a little eccentric', his personality being 'a peculiar mixture of the insufferable and the enchanting'.

He believed the years 1911–1914 were his most formative and rewarding period. *Bright Day*, for many devotees the favourite Priestley novel, and the most autobiographical, reflects those years, telling of a young man's enlightenment in the carefree years before the Great War, via a cultured and musical family with several lively daughters. In an early essay, Jack had written wistfully about a Yorkshire family, the Thorlaws, at whose hospitable house folks gathered. There Jack sang comic songs 'by the hour, without shame'. The people who thronged to the Thorlaws' were 'nothing like the beautiful, the clever, the distinguished persons whose acquaintance I can boast today' (he was writing this in 1927), 'but dimly consecrated in my memory by a happiness that something seems to have withered away, shining there in a queer kind of Golden Age, strangely compounded of provincial nobodies and cheap port and chaff and comic songs.'

But overshadowing *Bright Day* was foreboding as well as nostalgia. That Golden Age was summarily disrupted by the outbreak of World War I. In 1914, Jack volunteered with the 10th Duke of Wellington's West Riding battalion, of the 23rd division. He celebrated his twenty-first birthday on the front line, 'among shells and bloodstained barbed wire'. His experiences in the trenches 'when the guns began to roar and the corpses piled up' remained 'an open wound that never healed'. The Great War afflicted him deeply. He was luckier than the doughty lads who joined the Bradford 'Pals' battalion, 'the most eager, promising and finest members of my generation' who were butchered on the Somme on 1 July 1916. So he was deprived of most childhood friends ('The men that were boys when I was a boy are dead'), and he very nearly died himself. He never wrote of his experiences, but he read voraciously and observed human behaviour. 'Reunion Battalion Dinner' tells of his reunion in Bradford with survivors of his platoon, seventeen years on, in which he expresses his outrage that some old comrades were absent because they could not afford to pay for, or to dress for, such a reunion dinner.

Home from the trenches, Lieutenant John Priestley, aged twenty-four, took advantage of the ex-officer's grant to go to Cambridge, to read English literature at Trinity Hall, switching to history and political science. Cambridge did not dazzle him; he had 'left too many illusions flattened in the Flanders mud'. He could hardly enjoy undergraduate life on a grant that scarcely kept him alive. 'I had never felt really happy there, never even felt cosily at home.' The literary critic known as Q, Sir Arthur Quiller-Couch, tried to persuade him to stay on and teach, but he was 'too bloody-minded a fellow to fall in with academic life, or to take a teaching job'. Besides, he had already published his first book, *Brief Diversions*, 'a little book of undergraduate odds and ends'. His original goal was to rent a cottage on the edge of the moors, aiming to make twenty five shillings a week by his pen. But *Brief Diversions* prompted him to take his new wife Pat, already pregnant with their first daughter, to London 'with some vague introductions and capital of about forty seven pounds' and launch himself as a freelance. After all, he had sold his first piece to a London periodical as long ago as 1910. He would never live in the north again – but he never forgot his roots, and his ashes are buried at Hubberholme in Wharfedale, Yorkshire.

Living by his pen, he took to 1920s London: 'English life in brick, chimney pots, old squares, smoke and mist.' Financially, he became successful enough to inhabit London's more prosperous quarters – Kensington, the leafy heights of Hampstead and Highgate, and the exclusive enclave of Albany, Piccadilly. But he ended up in a country house in Alveston, Warwickshire, far from 'the intolerable strain of contemporary metropolitan living, the growing defeat of human zest and sympathy by the mere mechanics of existence.'

Looking back on how his writing career began, he realised that it all started with essays. 'I was rather clever, I now realise, at avoiding journalism and not becoming an employee.' Essays were still a flourishing market, despite being already 'almost an anachronism'. Periodicals such as *Lilliput*, the *Spectator*, the *Saturday Review*, the *Daily News* and the *London Mercury* were his outlets. 'I prefer a wide audience,' he said in his son

Tom's film. 'I aim for simplicity, not complicity. Something I could read aloud in a beer parlour.' He had a clear idea of his own readability, but never suggested that essay-writing was a facile exercise. Starting work always involved sitting down at one's desk and 'lifting the elephant off the typewriter'.

But in his early years in London he faced a real struggle when his young wife, pregnant with their second daughter, became seriously ill. In an essay called 'Dark Hours', he wrote of the night horrors of chronic insomnia, 'a glimpse of Hell' which afflicted him between 1924 and 1926. Sylvia, the miracle baby, was two months premature, the smallest ever to have survived in Guy's Hospital maternity wing. But then it was revealed that Pat had advanced cancer of the bladder. She was in no state to cope with two babies, and Priestley had to employ a cook-housekeeper. At the same time, he heard that Jonathan, his father – instinctive Socialist, born teacher, fell-walker, cricketer, amateur actor, pillar of chapel – was ill and frail at fifty-six, and proved to have stomach cancer. Priestley, burdened with medical bills, was 'half out of my mind with overwork and worry'. Pat died, aged twenty-nine, in 1925, leaving Barbara (almost three) and Sylvia (19 months) and Priestley at thirty-one a widower who had lost his boyhood friends and his father.

His output became prodigious: his first novel, *Adam in Moonshine* (1927), an apprentice work, which critics called 'an essayist's novel', was followed by a gothic novel, *Benighted*. He also published three collections of essays and two volumes on literary themes: *Figures of Modern Literature* and *English Comic Characters*. During this period of professional productivity and personal upheaval, Priestley also became involved with his second wife. He met the lively, handsome Jane Wyndham-Lewis at a literary party she gave with her husband Bevan. Jane, a graduate in modern languages from Bedford College, already had one daughter – named Barbara, like Jack's firstborn, so she had now to be known as Angela. Bevan Wyndham-Lewis was himself involved with another married woman; and when Jane left him for Priestley she was pregnant with their daughter Mary.

Fortunately, with a wife and four daughters to support, Priestley was about to become a man of substance. His most famous novels, *The Good Companions* (1929) and *Angel Pavement* (1931), sold 'by the lorryload', bringing prosperity. Jack and Jane moved from comfortable Victorian Well Walk, Hampstead, into a grand Georgian abode: a handsome nine-bedroomed house in The Grove, on the pinnacle of Highgate Hill, once the home of Coleridge, with a splendid garden overlooking Hampstead Heath. Coleridge's study became Priestley's, where he could play the piano. Tom, Priestley's only son, was born in 1932 when his father was on the verge of a new form of success, in the theatre: baby Tom attended rehearsals for *Dangerous Corner* in his carry-cot.

A succession of hit plays by Priestley dominated the London stage throughout the 1930s and 40s, and they prove their longevity by featuring still in the repertory: *Time and the Conways*, *When We Are Married* and *An Inspector Calls* being just three of them. But essay-writing continued. He might ponder on mortality (in 'Dissolution in Haymarket'), or on youth versus age (in 'On the Moors') or wax lyrical about something as basic as the humble household screw, prompting readers to note its beautiful simplicity and efficiency: when screwed in tight, a screw will hold a thing fast for fifty years. He lamented the Hollywood-style expressiveness of his face (in 'Different Inside'). 'My face would seem to belong to a type of man I dislike. It is a theatrical, temperamental affair, for ever rushing out to extremes, whereas I am all for moderation.'

By 1938, he was a distinguished enough essayist to be included in *English Essays of Today*, along with Hilaire Belloc, G. K. Chesterton, Max Beerbohm, E. V. Lucas and Sir Arthur Quiller-Couch, towering men of letters all, descendants of Addison, Hazlitt and Lamb. He was twenty years younger than any of the others, but Priestley's essay, 'First Snow' (from his first collection, *I For One*, 1923) is among the most memorable in the book, capturing the dramatic shock of an overnight snowfall: 'Outside the closed curtains of the bedroom, a vast transformation scene is taking place.' But readers will find *aperçu*s in every essay. 'There is always something peculiarly revolting and unnatural about a spectacled murderer.' 'If only our rulers might be photographed holding a book instead of patting a racehorse.' 'There are certain kinds of faces and figures – soldiers and policemen have them – that seem to belong to uniforms.' 'Schoolmasters never really retire; there is always, at the back of their minds, an unconquered, never-to-be-surrendered fortress of pedagogy.'

In the 1940s the broadcast talk began to replace the essay, 'and though I say it as shouldn't, I was a pretty good broadcaster,' Priestley reflected. In his twenty-eight wartime *Postscripts*, previously mentioned, he tried to express his hopes for a better world after the war. 'We should not be going back to the old England but forward to a new one' – an England with a sense of community, of 'being all in the same boat'. His deep warm voice struck just the right note with sixteen million listeners: the *Postcripts* provoked an alarming (to him) level of fame and adulation. People stopped him in the pub, wanted to shake his hand, wrote fan letters by the sackful. 'It got embarrassing. As soon as you get popular . . . complete strangers want to touch you,' he said, although he admitted he enjoyed letters from 'nice, intelligent and rather shy people'.

The *Postscripts*' overtly political stance also cast him into a political wilderness, persona non grata with both Right and Left. The BBC was censured in the House of Commons for airing his dangerously Red views, while he was revered in Russia, where *An*

Inspector Calls first opened in 1946: hence his first visit to Russia, with Jane, who told the children in letters home, 'They simply adore Daddy here . . . his books sell like hot cakes.' Although he had campaigned for the Labour party's landslide victory in 1945, he was persuaded to stand as an Independent for the Cambridge University seat, and was relieved not to win: 'To sit there, day after day, listening to all that rubbish.' His political colour was pink, 'and a pleasant healthy colour it is too'. Without a party allegiance, as his son says, 'he could say what he pleased'.

After 1945 he was even more engaged in the cause of building a better world. 'The British were absolutely at their best in the Second World War,' he later wrote. 'They were never as good, certainly in my lifetime before it, and I'm sorry to say I think never been quite as good after it.' But the society they built was bound to disappoint. By 1957 Priestley had become trenchantly partisan, writing often 'out of devilment' – 'blazing and crashing away in an attempt to strike sparks from the rock-like complacency of the English', as his first biographer Susan Cooper put it. The essay 'Eros and Logos', his guide to the opposing principles of Eros/ Yin/feminine, and Logos/Yang/masculine, is a critique of the irredeemable masculine values of America – 'restlessness, ruthless ambition . . . mechanical progress . . . idolatry of business'. (The first half of this essay would serve as a perfect manifesto for the Women's Equality Party founded by Sandi Toksvig in

2015.) 'Another Revolution' is his indictment of the power and rise of television. The highbrow popularity of cinema in the 1950s might outstrip the intellectual appeal of verse plays by Fry and Eliot, he observed, but it was clear that neither could compete with Television, which 'exists continually in a champagne atmosphere of ballyhoo and excitement that sound radio, even in its greatest days, never knew'.

The biggest upheaval in Priestley's life in the 1950s was his divorce from Jane in 1952 and his marriage to the archaeologist Jacquetta Hawkes, author of the recent bestselling masterpiece, *A Land*. (Happily, Jane too got married again, to the ornithologist David Bannerman.)

In October 1957, John Freeman at the *New Statesman* suggested an essay subject Priestley might tackle: Britain and the Nuclear Bombs. In it, he scornfully demolished pro-Bomb arguments about deterrence, and warned that in the 'idiot game' of playing with ultimate weapons of destruction, the players 'hag-ridden by fear' might push the wrong button after three glasses too many of vodka, or bourbon-on-the-rocks. Was civilisation bent on self-destruction? Although no pacifist, he told readers: 'Now that Britain has told the world she has the H-bomb, she should announce as early as possible that she has done with it, that she proposes to reject, in all circumstances, nuclear warfare.' The result was dramatic. Such an avalanche of readers' letters arrived at Great Turnstile, the *New Statesman* office, that it led to the foundation of CND. The letters were passed to the embryonic 'National Campaign Against Nuclear Weapons', whose meetings were held at 2 Amen Corner, home of Canon John Collins and his wife Diana, who became the Priestleys' lifelong friends. At first, both Jack and Jacquetta stamped across the country addressing CND meetings, and as vice-president, Priestley spoke at the first Aldermaston rally. Jacquetta continued to run the CND women's committee of female writers and scientists. But Priestley left the campaign over Bertrand Russell's squabbles about direct action. He never cared much for committees, or resolutions, or sit-ins.

Looking back on his prolific essay output, he was discerning. About half of them 'could be – and will be, unless a fire is handy – chucked into the waste paper basket'. He mocked his own tendency to go 'grumbling at large', and I have ditched much Grumpy Old Man huffing and puffing, as brilliantly satirised in Craig Brown's Wallace Arnold column in the *Independent*. (Wallace would rail against any tiresome innovations, such as windscreen wipers.) Priestley comes closest to self-parody in 'On Travel by Train', listing the iniquities of fellow passengers: the woman laden with noisy children or bulky shopping, passengers who feel they have to eat and drink, the tobacco-stained train-obsessed Bradshaw expert. 'I have sat, more than once, in a railway carriage,' Priestley wrote, 'with black murder in my heart.' Rail travel today would doubtless infuriate him even more, yet such essays date badly. Other themes still resonate with us – when he writes of municipal vandalism that transforms cities into vistas of concrete; or when he points out that 'people do not really want anything until they are told they want it'. He strikes chords when rhapsodising about modern recordings of Schubert's last and noblest work, the Quintet in C – 'which brings a gift so precious that it almost redeems the noise and idiocy of the time'.

As an honest scribbler, Priestley never deceived himself about his literary status. In a 1956 lecture, 'Literature in my Time', Dr F. R. Leavis rode roughshod over many reputations, declaring that 'life isn't long enough to permit one's giving much time to Fielding or any to Mr Priestley'. Jack responded in the *New Statesman* that the 'arrogantly dogmatic' Leavis might be right. 'But if our time is too precious to waste reading reputable authors from Fielding to Day-Lewis, why should we waste any time at all reading or listening to Dr Leavis?' Quite so. When Tom Priestley went up to Cambridge, and read English like his father but at King's College, he attended no lectures by Dr Leavis. His father visited him in Cambridge – once in a car driven by Ralph Richardson – but Tom felt he was steered by his father from taking up writing himself. He gravitated towards a much-overlooked profession: he became a celebrated, award-winning film editor, noted for films such as *Deliverance, Morgan: A Suitable Case for Treatment, The Great Gatsby* and much else.

Priestley never longed to decamp to foreign shores – despite being an inveterate traveller with a surprising enthusiasm for the Arizona Desert – and certainly not to the Mediterranean, which had 'too many damned olives'. He did not share the view 'that anything that happens in a foreign country is more romantic, charming, intelligent, gracious, than anything that happens at home'. And in an essay called 'Offshore Island Man' (1967) he made a cogent argument opposing our membership of the Common Market.

By the time he assembled the brief essays in *Particular Pleasures* (1975), on his favourite paintings, music and performers, Priestley could drop the names of practitioners of all the arts who were his personal acquaintances. One was Dame Peggy Ashcroft, with whom he had had a passionate affair in the early years of his second marriage. 'Of all leading actresses she might be said to be the least actressy,' he wrote, fondly remembering 'innumerable hours of talk with her' on matters other than the theatre. And Dame Sybil Thorndike was a dear friend: 'I once said she was more enthusiastic about everything than I was about anything.'

Priestley refused a knighthood, turned down the Companion of Honour and a peerage from Harold Wilson, being opposed to the Labour government's support for the American bombing of Vietnam. But he did accept the freedom of the City of Bradford, and in 1977 the Order of Merit, conferred by the Queen. His reputation, like that of most writers, has been subject to the vagaries of fashion. In the 1950s Priestley's plays faded along with those of Rattigan and Coward and other masters of 'the well-made play'. To that taunt, Priestley would retort, 'You wouldn't mock a table for being well-made, would you?' In *Look Back in Anger* (1956), John Osborne's anti-hero Jimmy Porter is caught reading Priestley in the *New Statesman* and dismisses it as 'Edwardian nostalgia'. Priestley responded by pointing out flaws in Osborne's play: what childless young woman would be ironing on a Sunday evening?

Susan Cooper predicted that Priestley's true worth was not likely to emerge until perhaps fifty years after his death. That would bring us to 2034. But in 2006, in a preface to a new edition of *Bright Day*, a chorus of voices contributed their thoughts on 'What Priestley means to Me' including the late Denis Healey, Michael Foot, Beryl Bainbridge, Alan Plater, Stan Barstow. Among the living, Margaret Drabble, Melvyn Bragg, Alan Ayckbourn, Tim West, Paul Johnson, David Hockney, Barry Cryer. In 2015, Alan Bennett, fellow West Riding writer, reflected on Priestley in his diary printed in the *London Review of Books*, February 2016, after watching a new TV production of *An Inspector Calls*. 'It's a play I'd dearly love to have written (as also his *When We Are Married*),' he wrote, 'and gives me a pang of conscience. Back in the late 1990s when I was doing some programmes on Westminster Abbey the dean, Michael Mayne, talked to me about whether

Larkin should be in Poets' Corner, an obvious yes on the strength of "Church Going" let alone the rest. He also wanted my thoughts on another candidate, J. B. Priestley, whom several supporters were pushing but on whom Michael M. wasn't keen. I hedged, I think, certainly not pressing Priestley's claim which on the evidence of tonight's *An Inspector Calls* fills me with regret and self-reproach.'

Bennett was not alone in that self-reproach. Many who paid tribute on J. B. Priestley's 75th birthday – when Sir Kenneth Clark and Dame Iris Murdoch were among the speakers at the Savoy dinner – hinted that he had not yet had the credit due to him. People had never known how to summarise this substantial figure with an infinite range: a man of letters who could write anything. On the facade of Number 3, The Grove, Highgate, there are two plaques: one states that here the poet Coleridge died in 1834 aged 61. The other says that 100 years later here lived J. B. Priestley, 'Novelist, playwright, essayist.' So posterity acknowledged not only the novels and plays but also a remarkable talent for a little-sung genre: the essay.

Highgate, 2016

– On Beginning –

1923

How difficult it is to make a beginning. I speak of essay-writing, an essentially virtuous practice, and not of breaking the ten commandments. It is much easier to begin, say, a review or an article than it is to begin an essay, for with the former you attach yourself to something outside yourself, you have an excuse for writing and therefore have more courage. If it is a review that has to be written, well, there, waiting for you, inviting your comment, is the book. Similarly with an article, you have your subject, something that everybody is excited about, let us say the Education of Correlates or the Bearing of Teleology on the Idea of God, and thus you know what is expected of you and (though it may sound difficult to common sense and physiology) you can take up your pen with a light heart. But to have nothing to cling hold of, to have no excuse for writing at all, to be compelled to spin everything out of oneself, to stand naked and shivering in the very first sentence one puts down, is clearly a very different matter, and this is the melancholy situation in which the essayist always finds himself. It is true that he need not always be melancholy; if he is full of himself, brimming over with bright talk, in a mood to take the whole world into his confidence, ready to rhapsodize about music-halls to Mr Bertrand Russell, Dean Inge, and the Lord Chief Justice, or to soliloquize on death and the mutability of things before the Mayor and Corporation of Stockport, if he is in such good fettle the essayist will find his task a very pleasant one indeed, never to be exchanged for such drudge's work as reviews and articles; and he will step briskly on to the stage and posture in the limelight without a tremor. But such moments are rare, and the essayist at ordinary times, though he would eagerly undertake to defend his craft, cannot quite rid himself of the feeling that there is something both absurd and decidedly impudent in this business of talking about oneself for money; this feeling haunts the back of his mind like some gibbering spectre, and it generally produces one of three effects. According to his temperament, it will prevent him from doing anything at all that particular day or perhaps any other day, or it will allow him to write a few brilliant opening sentences and then shut up, or it will keep him from making a start until the last possible moment.

For my own part, I am one of those who find it difficult to begin; I stand on the brink for hours, hesitating to make the plunge; I will do anything but the work in hand. This habit is certainly a nuisance, but perhaps it is not quite so intolerable as that of some other persons, men of my acquaintance, who fall into the second category mentioned above and always find themselves making dashing openings and then coming to a stop. Without a moment's hesitation, they will take up their pens and write on the top of a clean sheet of paper – 'On Massacre', and will then begin at once: 'It is only as a means to an end that Massacre can be adversely criticized. As an end in itself, something that is its own reward, there is nothing to be said against it and everything to be said for it. It is only since the gradual overclouding of the purely aesthetic view of life that Massacre has come to need any defence. It is true that we still talk of art, but actually we care nothing for its values, and in particular for those of Sublime Art, which asks for the whole of life upon which to experiment. Thus it is that we have come to misunderstand Massacre, a manifestation of the Sublime, and have lost sight of the true Herod.' At this point, they will stare at what they have written, well pleased with it as an opening, and then discover that the flow has ceased. They will write 'Albigenses' – 'Sicilian Vespers' – 'St Bartholomew' on the nearest sheet of blotting-paper, but all to no purpose; they will have come to a stop, and horrible hours will pass, and perhaps many more dashing openings will have been made, before any real progress will have come about and their essay taken some sort of shape. Such writers seem to me even more unfortunate than I am, for I do at least go forward once I have made a beginning; as soon as I have summoned up courage to ring the bell I am at least admitted into the house of my choice, and am not, like these others, left kicking my heels in the vestibules of half a dozen houses perhaps without ever seeing the interior of any of them.

Nevertheless, though there may be worse things, my own habit of procrastination is undoubtedly a great nuisance. Fear, indolence, and a plain incapacity to concentrate for more than a few seconds, all play their parts. In the end, it is true, they delay my beginning so long that they succeed in destroying themselves, for I become so desperate at last that my fear and indolence are willy-nilly driven out of court and I even achieve some sort of concentration. But in the meantime I have wasted hours and hours. I begin, usually in the morning, with the fullest intention of settling down immediately to work; an essay has to be written; it has been left too long already, and I have no time to waste. But no sooner have I arrived in my room than I begin to do a great many things that I never do at any other time. I clean a pipe or two, all the while pretending to myself that I am eager to get to work, though it is curious (to say the least of it) that I never scrape and clean my pipes at any other time. After having lovingly filled and lighted one of these beautifully clean pipes, I sit down, but get up again almost immediately to straighten one of the pictures, to restore a few books to their proper shelves, or to clear away any odd papers that may be lying about. Then instead of sitting at my table on a hard little chair, whose unyielding surface and ungracious angles would serve to remind me that life is real and earnest, I bury myself in an enormous basket-chair of the kind that is exceedingly popular (and not without good reason) at the universities. This chair is so long and low that I always find it necessary to have my feet off the ground when I am sitting in it, so in this thoroughly comfortable posture, with slippered feet up somewhere near the fire-place, knees slightly bent, head well back, I prepare myself to grapple with the work in hand. I reach for my fountain-pen and a stiff writing-pad; my pipe is going beautifully; now, if ever, is the time to concentrate. But alas! – I cannot concentrate. I can follow another man's thought, in a book or out of it, as long as it should be necessary, but left to its own devices my mind does nothing but wander aimlessly, for I am of a discursive habit of mind, with strong but eccentric powers of association. Mr Pelman and his friends would weep over my puling attempts to keep my thought to its proper theme; and I sometimes think that I would seek their assistance had I not somewhere at the back of my mind a fear that they would contrive to turn me away from scribbling altogether and convert me to Salesmanship, whatever that may be.

Gloriously at ease, then, lying in my big fat chair, I consider the prose masterpiece in miniature that must be born into the world during these next few hours. In bed last night, when I ought to have been asleep, I had the whole thing worked out; it was there down to the last comma, and it was wonderful; the bed-posts

were festooned with noble thoughts and the counter-
pane glittered with bright miraculous phrases; there
can be no doubt that I surpassed myself last night. No
wonder that now, when the work has actually to be
done, I feel so sleepy. And unfortunately, though the
subject itself remains, I can hardly remember a word
of what I invented last night, and the few snatches I do
remember seem crude and thin. It does not even appear a very promising subject now. What is there to be
said about it that has not already been said? Little or
nothing. But something must be done, so I write down
the title and draw a line underneath it, and contrary to
my usual practice I do this very slowly and carefully,
merely to waste time and retard the evil moment when
I shall have to take thought. But long before I have finished drawing the line, my mind has wandered whole
continents away from the subject. Drawing the line so
slowly has made me think of an old master I once had
at school who was always pointing out that the best
way to draw straight lines without the aid of a ruler
was to draw them very quickly; and from him my mind
has rambled round to other masters I had, and from
them to holidays, and to friends and California and
paintbrushes and Whistler and Chelsea and my friend
X and Devonshire cream and finally to Coleridge. And
now that I have arrived at Coleridge, I suddenly remember that I want to look up some passage in the
Table-Talk, so with a not ignoble effort I scramble out
of my chair and search for the book and the particular

passage. And now it is nearly half an hour since I read that passage, but the *Table-Talk* is still in my hands and I am still reading. But I put it down because I recollect an old project of mine, a book on the criticism of Coleridge, and now I begin to plan that book all over again and detached phrases for the introductory chapter come into my mind; and now I decide that I must sketch my plan for this book on paper, and I take up my pen and paper again, but only to remember that I have an essay to write. . . . Lunch has come and gone. . . . And now I will settle down and get my work done. But first I must put away the copy of Coleridge's *Table-Talk* still lying in my chair. So I put it away, but when I withdraw my hand it has taken out the second volume of Leslie Stephen's *Hours in a Library,* and for no accountable reason I find myself still standing by the bookshelf reading his essay on Horace Walpole. This will never do, and rather angrily I put Stephen away and fling myself down in my chair once more. My manhood is at stake; I must take the plunge; so without more ado I seize hold of my pen and paper and write: 'How difficult it is to make a beginning. I speak of essay-writing, an essentially virtuous practice, and not of breaking the ten commandments . . .' And then, with only a few halts, I go forward to the end. But what the end is, I cannot tell you, for it has all become very complicated.

– A Coincidence –

1923

Although we talk so much about coincidence, we do not really believe in it. In our heart of hearts, we think better of the universe; we are secretly convinced that it is not such a slipshod haphazard affair, that everything in it has a meaning. If, let us say, a man rises on New Year's morning, takes up his newspaper, and, opening it casually, finds himself staring at a name identical with his own in the column of Deaths, it is a thousand to one that he will be shocked and strangely apprehensive. Afterwards, he will relate the incident to his friends, call it a curious coincidence, and laugh, loudly though not heartily, over it, and his friends will call it a curious coincidence too, and they will all laugh loudly together and slap one another on the back and feel convinced that they are fine strong fellows with no nonsense about them. This, at least, is what the men will do; the women, who are realists and less given to deluding themselves, will be more openly dubious. None of them will feel entirely comfortable at heart; they will all find it difficult to dismiss the notion that somehow or other such an incident is significant, that behind it lies the finger not of chance but of fate.

As we go through the year we light upon quite a

number of these 'coincidences' that we choose to inter-
pret one way or the other; and whether they promise
good or ill fortune, it is certain that they always promise
something. Even the smallest, things so trifling that we
do not consider them worth mentioning to our friends,
are not without their effect. The old wondering, peering, superstitious creature that crouches at the back
of all our minds sees them as light straws borne along
the wind of fortune. Even the most trifling of all will
yet induce a mood, a mood that may lead to a quarrel
or a reconciliation, to the revocation of a will or the
beginning of a masterpiece. It is very foolish and even
dangerous to imagine that we are reasonable beings;
such notions, in view of what we think we know of the
history of our species, are themselves highly unreasonable. So it will do us little harm openly to confess for
once the quite irrational influence that certain curious
incidents, sometimes spoken of as coincidences, have
upon our minds. If it is a weakness, it is probably a
universal one, and so need not trouble anyone.

Having thus, rather cunningly I think, put everybody into the same boat, I am ready to admit what I
should not admit without some such preamble. I am
ready to admit that I have been oddly troubled for the
past week by the memory of a very absurd little coincidence. Unhappily it was not a pleasant one; it has left
a nasty flavour in the mouth; and though nothing may
come of it (for I cannot really see that it has any recog-
nizable significance) I do not feel so sure of myself as I

did. Something, I feel, is rotten, somewhere, and I can only hope that it is still in the state of Denmark. What I call a coincidence insists upon assuming, somewhere in the darker regions of my mind, the form of an accusation, until I feel vaguely responsible for all manner of evils, like a man who imagines that he has done murder in his sleep.

Last week, I was staying in the north of England, and set out one day to visit an old friend of mine who lives in one of those little industrial places, half towns, half villages, that are to be found in the neighbourhood of the great manufacturing cities. This particular village is perched on the summit of a hill and lies on the edge of a wide moor. It is a grim, forbidding country, bleak and desolate before the coming of the tall factories, and still more inhuman and terrifying to the eyes of a stranger now that its surface is pockmarked with the unlovely signs of industry, looking as if the great hills had broken into small-pox. The factories thrust up their long slender chimneys and show their thousand and one windows, like blind eyes, to the cold light; the few green fields are harshly framed in black walls; great cinder heaps abound there; monotonous rows of little houses run sharply this way and that, up or down from the dirty roads; in front are the brown wastes of moorland, with their scattered lumps of hard jagged black rock silhouetted against the sky. The moors frown on the mills, and the mills frown on the men. Such country cannot be ignored; it grips hold of the mind; it is unique. Human nature being by no means a tender plant, it flowers there as elsewhere; indeed, this part of England is a great breeding ground for massive virtues and odd humours.

Only at night does it become tolerable to a stranger. On a fine clear night, all its harshness disappears, and it achieves an unfamiliar beauty of its own. When the sun has finally gone down, a few strange lights, pale amethyst, green, deep orange, linger above the moorland. The hills fade into the sky; the distant tram-cars, climbing the hills, look like shining golden beetles; the street-lamps across the valley seem to bring new and pretty constellations into the sky. Unhappily, it was not night when I boarded a tram-car that would take me to my friend's ugly village on the hill, and though a tram ride there is rather exciting, for the track is almost that of a mountain railway, and the trams are like top-heavy creaky galleons, I felt depressed as I stared out of the window. The tram made one last groaning effort and succeeded in scaling the rise that leads to the village. We passed mournful and ill-shaped football grounds, groups of little allotment gardens, sufficiently unlovely to smirch the innocence even of a vegetable, and what was worst, any number of those hideous little hen-runs in which the submerged tenth of the race of fowls peck out a miserable existence. We passed a public-house or two, and then were soon into the village. I remarked the dreary little shops, the short streets that ran sharply down from one side of the road, and the houses, built of stone and now nearly black. The tram stopped and I descended into the street, in no humour for an encounter with the representative of any lower civilization, such as a bland Chinaman or a tall smiling South Sea Islander.

Facing me, as I descended from the tram, was a little street that immediately attracted my attention. It had only four or five houses on each side, almost windowless dwellings with the colour and lines of coal trucks. They had no gardens, nor even yards, railings or a few steps; the hapless folk who lived in them walked straight from the street into the house or from the house into the street. Only a small part of the roadway was paved, the rest being a dreadful mixture of grass, cinders and mire. It ended in a patch of waste ground, from which the grass had long been worn. There was the road at the top, with the trams groaning by, and the patch of waste ground at the bottom, and the two little rows of dark cottage houses looking at each other. There seemed to be no children there, or cats and dogs, or even open doors: nothing but an unbroken silence. It seemed to me, as I stood there, to be the most unpleasant street I had ever seen, the very last street in the world I would ever choose to live in. It was not one of your picturesque, lurid slum streets, ever ripe for either a spree or a murder; it was perfectly respectable, and always would be; no Sunday newspaper would ever make good copy out of its doings; it kept itself to itself. But what a place, inconceivably dreary, suffocating! Everything that had gone to make that street was clearly wrong; there could be no argument about it, no question of this system or that system; something stood plainly indicted. There behind those walls, living and loving, dwelt Man, the dream of the swarming protozoa, how noble in reason, how infinite in faculties!

But what of the coincidence that has disturbed me in secret for this past week? Why, at that moment, when I had just begun to mutter 'There, but for the grace of God . . .,' it suddenly occurred to me to look for the name of this street, fully expecting to discover in it some last ironical stroke, some mention of Lavender, Acacia or even Paradise. I looked up, and there, above my head and plain for all the world to see, was the name in bold white letters – Priestley Street.

– All About Ourselves –

1923

'Now tell me,' said the lady, 'all about yourself.' The effect was instantaneous, shattering. Up to that moment, I had been feeling expansive; I was self-confident, alert, ready to give a good account of myself in the skirmish of talk. If I had been asked my opinion of anything between here and Sirius, I would have given it at length, and I was quite prepared to talk of places I had never seen and books I had never read; I was ready to lie, and to lie boldly and well. Had she not made that fatal demand, I would have roared like the sweet little lion she imagined me to be, roared as gently as any sucking-dove or nightingale: for, unlike that haphazard impresario Peter Quince, I had, you may say, 'the lion's part written'. But to tell her all about myself. My expansive mood suddenly shrivelled to nothing; every richly dyed shred of personality was stripped from me and there remained only my naked, shivering mortality. Nothing but a jumble of memorable old phrases haunted my mind: I was, like Socrates in the first syllogism, a man and therefore a mortal, such stuff as dreams are made on, born of a woman and full of trouble, one whose days are as grass . . . What was there to be said? I stared at my sprightly companion, who was still smiling, half- playfully, half-expectantly, and I must have looked like a child peering from the ruins at the squadrons of an invading army. Then I mumbled something so unsatisfactory that, despairing of any intimate avowals, she passed on to some other topic, while I, donning my cloak and wig, my cap and bells, left the naked six feet of ground to which her demand had confined me, and made haste to follow her. Yorick was himself again.

The request, so framed, was undoubtedly preposterous. Indeed, it was so obviously calculated to silence any normal human being that one may reasonably suspect the motive that lay behind it. To confess one's terror at meeting such a demand is not necessarily to hint at an engaging modesty. It was so all-embracing, so ultimate, that only a megalomaniac or a great genius could have coped with it. A request to know what I had been doing for the past year or intended to do in the next twelve months, to know whether I approved of William Shakespeare or liked early rising, would have set my tongue wagging for an insufferable length of time. I am ready to talk about myself, that is, about my opinions, my likes and dislikes, my whims, my experiences, my hopes and fears, at any and every season. I have my own share of that windy, foolish, but, I hope, not too unpleasant vanity which is common to most people who do little tricks with words and pigments and fiddle-strings; I can fly my little coloured balloons of conceit with the next scribbler or chorus girl or cabinet minister. But even if we only need the merest shadow of an excuse to talk about ourselves, there must be something interposed between the universe and our bare selves; there must be bounds assigned to our flow of egotism; we must be given some idea of ourselves to work upon, to build up or knock down. To tell *all* about ourselves in one vast breath is really to press the whole round world in the lemon-squeezer of our minds, to explain the sum total of things in terms of ourselves, to raise the ego to a monstrous height. The very thought of it flips the mind with 'a three-man beetle' and stuns a man into humility.

Perhaps with most men there comes a time when they are able to give a reasonable sort of account of themselves; but I, for one, am free to confess that I have not yet travelled so far. I am still busy trying, un-successfully as yet, to piece together the various im-pressions and opinions of myself I gather from other people to make up the fragments of my portrait. I am still noting, with amazement, the broken reflections and queer glimpses of myself that I catch sight of in other people's minds. This I conceive to be the third stage of one's progress in self-knowledge: how long it lasts and whether there is a fourth stage at all are ques-tions that I cannot answer. But I can vouch for the two previous stages. When we are very young, not only has the earth and every common sight (to plunder Words-worth) the glory and the freshness of a dream, but we ourselves have something of the same glory and fresh-

ness; we gulp experience and do not question ourselves, and this golden age lasts until we realize, with
something of a shock, that there are other selves who
see us from the outside just as we see them. It is when
we become conscious of other selves that we become
self-conscious. Then we pass on to the second, most
disquieting stage, which, for most people who are im-
pressionable and imaginative, covers the whole period
of their later teens and early twenties, and may even
last considerably longer.

At this time we do nothing but question ourselves;
rosy little Hamlets, we are for ever busy with self-
communion. Never are we so anxious to discover what
we are and never do we make so little of the matter as
we do then. We examine ourselves in the light of everything we read, and become weathercocks swinging
before the changing wind of ideas. An hour of Swin-
burne turns us into magnificent pagans and sensuous
lovers, but before the day is out, a few pages of Carlyle
have promptly transformed us into sturdy philosophers
or roaring men of action. We can be Stoics before
breakfast, Epicureans after lunch, and uncertain but
hopeful Platonists before nightfall. Then gradually we
lose heart, for though every philosophy attracts us and
seems to have been almost designed to catch our eye,
though we can always read so much of ourselves into
every character we admire, yet there is always something essential wanting in us. We might he anything:
we are nothing; nothing but a bundle of impulses, a

ragbag of discarded ideals and wavering loyalties. We are convinced that other people will never understand us, will never be subtle enough to appreciate that curious quality which, for all our wretched lack of anything like character, our instability of purpose, our wandering will, somehow makes us splendid and unique. Meanwhile, we can make nothing of ourselves, for we seem radically different from hour to hour, according to the company we are in. If we are with some great lout of a fellow, then we see ourselves dapper, fragile, precious, and, in a flash, decide the path we will take for the rest of our lives. But no sooner do we fall in with some little dandy than we hear our own voices, cutting through his mincing accents, and recognize in them the notes of strong determined men who will make their way in the world. So we go on, until we feel that we can show nothing to the world but this dance of shifting selves.

But we grow up, and then either we cast off introspection in engaging to do the world's work or we still try to puzzle it all out. Perhaps we begin to remark the figures we cut in the minds of our friends and acquaintances, and try to live up to the best of them; though how we discover which are the best of them is a question I am not prepared to answer. This may lead us into vanity, a swelling eager sort of vanity, restless in pursuit of praise, a characteristic that is not so bad as it sounds. As some wiser men have already pointed out, vanity is at least warm, human, social, frankly dependent upon sympathy. There is an infinitely worse alternative, easy to fall into if we strongly approve of ourselves and yet shrink from soliciting other people's suffrages, and this is the solitary and desolating vice of pride. Many a man is praised for his reserve and so-called shyness when he is simply too proud to risk making a fool of himself. The vain man will cut capers in order to obtain notice and applause, the proud man asks for notice and applause without being willing to cut the capers, while the very proud man has such a miraculous self that he does not even want the applause. Some philosophies make this last state of complete self-satisfaction their goal, but one and all omit to mention the obvious advantages enjoyed by the oyster on such a plan of life. But unless we are victims of such icy folly, we discover, perhaps to our astonishment, that our greatest moments come when we find that we are not unique, when we come upon another self that is very like our own. The discovery of a continent is mere idle folly compared with this discovery of a sympathetic other-self, a friend or a lover. Where now is the sickly pleasure in not being understood, in being unique, miraculous, entirely self-satisfying, in shutting the painted doors and windows of the mind? Before this solid smashing happiness of thus being understood, all our walls go down and the sunlight comes streaming in. And then, and not until then, begins that endless tale which seems to be merely about this and that, but is really all about ourselves.

– Having Covered the Card Table –

E verybody agreed that the card table needed a new covering. In place of that smooth green sward which makes the tournament of hearts and spades a delight to the eye, our card table had long been showing us a field that looked like some dreary recreation ground in a little industrial town, all faded, patchy, grey, fit for nothing better than sixes of clubs. There was talk of calling in the local carpenter, but I would not hear of it. I told them I would do it myself. They were surprised, humorous, indulgent, but I persisted. I had already examined the table and had come to the conclusion that it would furnish me with a pleasant little job, well within my very limited range of craftsmanship. The sides, which apparently held in position the baize or felt (actually it is felt, though everybody thinks it is baize), were screwed on, so that they could easily be removed, and the old cloth torn off and the new tacked on without much difficulty. I was not to be defrauded of so much happy screwing and tacking, so much stretching of smooth bright green cloth, by any bored artisan. I bought some felt and came hurrying back with it almost as if it were some new music or a parcel of books, and then, having surrounded myself with screwdrivers, scissors, hammers, tacks, pipes, tobacco, and matches, I spent a solidly happy morning.

It is very odd that I should thus find myself more and more interested in working with my hands. I would seem to have reversed the usual progress in the hobbies of men, who commonly begin with the boy's carpentering outfit (complete on card) and gradually find their way to books and ideas. When I was a boy, however, I hated handiwork, and cared for nothing but books and games. The *Boy's Own Paper* showered instructions on me in vain, and I could pass by the most glorious set of tools, rows of gleaming chisels and gouges, without a thrill. No lop-sided boat of my laborious creation ever waddled out from the shore to heel over in the middle of the park lake or village pond. I never made anything and did not possess even a pocket-knife. Christmas and birthdays brought me books, footballs, cricket-bats, single-sticks, and the like, and the only time I ever received anything to build up (it was a gigantic loop-the-loop contrivance, made up of hundreds and hundreds of little pieces of stiff cardboard: my father finally erected it), I was disgusted. At one high school that I attended for a season there was a period set aside for what was called 'manual work', when pencil-boxes and iron paper-weights came clumsily and mournfully into being, and this period was a misery to me, whose shapeless bits of wood and pieces of battered metal were for ever held up to derision. In all other matters but this of craftsmanship, I was the

conventional boy, a ferocious fullback, a slogging bats-
man, a rapturous student of pantomime, good for three
helpings of suet pudding, but for the rest I preferred
the inside of a book to the inside of a steam engine and
never even touched a hammer if I could avoid it.

When I say that I bought my first box of tools only
a few years ago, a light will be thrown on my curious
history. It seems as if I am becoming more and more
interested in those things that I neglected in my boyhood. Nowadays I like to know why the wheels go
round. I have something of a passion, if not an openly
declared one, for what my friend the etcher happily
calls 'gadgetry'. I have not only mended a gramophone
and a typewriter, but am frequently to be found boast-
ing about it. As yet I have not achieved a workshop,
but I am rapidly becoming one of those men who do
the little jobs about the house. By the time I am an
old man, I shall probably be completely indifferent to
books, having taken to fretwork and Meccano sets. As
a craftsman, I am still a blundering novice, but the enthusiasm is there and time will ripen all. My planing is
still contemptible; my sawing is weak; but my screwing
and nailing are now almost up to professional standard, being sure, cool, masterful. This covering of the
card table was my opportunity, for there were fourteen
trim screws to be taken out and put in again, and tacks
innumerable to hold the smooth green felt in position. It would be hard to say which gives me the more
pleasure, the tack, that little epigram of the nailbox,

demanding only a tiny push with the finger and then a jolly crack with the hammer, or the screw, so subtle and so enduring, with its initial outburst of wilfulness followed by its gradual submission, until at last it seems to conquer the material almost of its own accord.

Perhaps, though, the screw gives us the finer pleasure. I enjoyed every moment with those fourteen, enjoyed their brief effort at resistance, their crescendo of easy exit, their snug reentry. Compelled as I am to deal so largely in human stuff, is it to be wondered at that I should find such delight in screws? I spend my days poring over the records of men's thoughts and dreams, wondering at their courage and timidity and impudence and vanity, praising here and blaming there, losing myself in the shadowy Walpurgis Night that we call literature. I see my fellow-creatures pretending to be better and wiser than they are or more base and foolish, counterfeiting emotions they have never really known or hiding feelings that have shaken them for years. I spend hours and hours spinning theories or absorbing some other man's ideas, only to find, on looking back, that all is moonshine. I take mind and heart to this subject and that, pour myself out and then wrestle with the stubborn sheets, yet at the end I do not know whether anything has been created, whether it is not all idle vanity. There are perhaps a few moments of intense satisfaction for me while the work is in hand; there is a brief delight in the turning of a dangerous corner; and then nothing but fret and labour that is at once hard and yet fantastic until the work is done and I am free to juggle lazily with the next dream. If I get no praise for what I have done, then I am heartsick; but if praise does come my way, then it seems to me foolish and ful-some and I am irritated or embarrassed. So it goes on. This way of life is my own choice and I would have no other, not even though I should have my 'yachts and string quartets'; but sometimes there is a joy in taking leave of it, in stretching green felt across the top of a card table, in turning home a good solid screw.

With a screw, biting its way into the woodwork and staying there if need be for half a century or, if you will, returning to your hand, the very same screw, within the next five minutes, you know where you are. It was devised for one kind of work, and that work it will do. It cheats neither itself nor you, is as definite, as rigid, as this other stuff with which I commonly deal in shifty and shadowy, maliciously protean. When you have tightened the last of your handful of screws, you can survey your work with solid contentment: some-thing new has been created, if only the cover of a card table, and its existence cannot be argued away. My screwing and scissoring and hammering are done, and now our shining kings and queens and knaves have a new smooth lawn for their strange encounters. A man with such jobs to do daylong, measuring the work with a wise eye, now taking up his screwdriver, now his scis-sors, now his hammer, is in no bad case, if, that is, he has enough in his pocket at the day's end for his steak and beer and baccy and occasional visit to the play. A man so situated is a churl if he grumbles. On the other hand, if he is bundled into a roaring great factory and there has to pass the whole day holding or cutting the felt, or hammering in tacks, or putting screws in holes while another man turns the screwdriver, then we can hardly blame him if he comes to the conclusion that he is being cheated, if he turns into a man with a grievance. He thinks that he is being cheated out of money, but whether he is or not, the fact remains that he is certainly being cheated out of something even more important, namely, a decent and amusing job, that honest and engrossing work which is also great fun. There was a time when all work was of the kind that most of us at some time or other have performed purely to amuse ourselves, just as I covered the card table: we have – I speak for both sexes – dug up gardens, mown grass, picked fruit, woven and dyed cloth, sailed boats, made shelves and cupboards, knitted stockings, soled boots, cut down trees, printed books, and so forth. But I have yet to meet anybody who went to work in a factory for fun, who spent his leisure in taking part in mass production. The world will not be happy when all the economists have agreed together and have regimented us into equal hours and equal wages, but when everybody has more work, real work to do, when we are all happily covering card tables through the long day and have just leisure enough for an odd rubber or two before we go to bed.

– First Snow –

1928

M r Robert Lynd once remarked of Jane Austen's characters: 'They are people in whose lives a slight fall of snow is an event.' Even at the risk of appearing to this witty and genial critic as another Mr Woodhouse, I must insist that last night's fall of snow here was an event. I was nearly as excited about it this morning as the children, whom I found all peering through the nursery window at the magic outside and chattering as excitedly as if Christmas had suddenly come round again. The fact is, however, that the snow was as strange and enchanting to me as it was to them. It is the first fall we have had here this winter, and last year I was out of the country, broiling in the tropics, during the snowy season, so that it really does seem an age since I saw the ground so fantastically carpeted. It was while I was away last year that I met the three young girls from British Guiana who had just returned from their first visit to England. The two things that had impressed them most were the endless crowds of people in the London streets, all strangers (they emphasized this, for they had spent all their lives in a little town where everybody knew everybody) and the snow-covered landscape they awoke to one morning when they were staying somewhere in Somerset. They were so thrilled and delighted that they flung away any pretence of being demure young ladies and rushed out of the house to run to and fro across the glittering white expanses, happily scattering footmarks on the untrodden surface, just as the children did in the garden this morning.

The first fall of snow is not only an event but it is a magical event. You go to bed in one kind of world and wake up to find yourself in another quite different, and if this is not enchantment, then where is it to be found? The very stealth, the eerie quietness, of the thing makes it more magical. If all the snow fell at once in one shattering crash, awakening us in the middle of the night, the event would be robbed of its wonder. But it flutters down, soundlessly, hour after hour while we are asleep. Outside the closed curtains of the bedroom, a vast transformation scene is taking place, just as if myriad elves and brownies were at work, and we turn and yawn and stretch and know nothing about it. And then, what an extraordinary change it is! It is as if the house you are in had been dropped down in another continent. Even the inside, which has not been touched, seems different, every room appearing smaller and cosier, just as if some power were trying to turn it into a woodcutter's hut or a snug log-cabin. Outside, where the garden was yesterday, there is now a white and glistening level, and the village beyond is no longer your own familiar cluster of roofs but a village in an old German fairy tale. You would not be surprised to learn that all the people there, the spectacled postmistress, the cobbler, the retired schoolmaster, and the rest, had suffered a change too and had become queer elvish beings, purveyors of invisible caps and magic shoes. You yourselves do not feel quite the same people you were yesterday. How could you when so much has been changed? There is a curious stir, a little shiver of excitement, troubling the house, not unlike the feeling there is abroad when a journey has to be made. The children, of course, are all excitement, but even the adults hang about and talk to one another longer than usual before settling down to the day's work. Nobody can resist the windows. It is like being on board ship.

When I got up this morning the world was a chilled hollow of dead white and faint blues. The light that came through the windows was very queer, and it contrived to make the familiar business of splashing and shaving and brushing and dressing very queer too. Then the sun came out, and by the time I had sat down to breakfast it was shining bravely and flushing the snow with delicate pinks. The dining-room window had been transformed into a lovely Japanese print. The little plum-tree outside, with the faintly flushed snow lining its boughs and artfully disposed along its trunk, stood in full sunlight. An hour or two later everything was a cold glitter of white and blue. The world had completely changed again. The little Japanese prints had all vanished. I looked out of my study window, over the garden, the meadow, to the low hills beyond, and the ground was one long glare, the sky was steely, and all the trees so many black and sinister shapes. There was indeed something curiously sinister about the whole prospect. It was as if our kindly countryside, close to the very heart of England had been turned into a cruel steppe. At any moment, it seemed, a body of horsemen might be seen breaking out from the black copse, so many instruments of tyranny, and shots might be heard and some distant patch of snow be reddened. It was that kind of landscape.

Now it has changed again. The glare has gone and no touch of the sinister remains. But the snow is falling heavily, in great soft flakes, so that you can hardly see across the shallow valley, and the roofs are thick and the trees all bending, and the weathercock of the village church, still to be seen through the grey loaded air, has become some creature out of Hans Andersen. From my study, which is apart from the house and faces it, I can see the children flattening their noses against the nursery window, and there is running through my head a jangle of rhyme I used to repeat when I was a child and flattened my nose against the cold window to watch the falling snow:

Snow, snow faster:
White alabaster!
Killing geese in Scotland,
Sending feathers here!

This, I fancy, must have been a north-country charm (for that grey upland region is full of wizardries) to bring down the snow. And though we are told by the experts that as much snow falls now as ever it did, we know better, and I suspect that the reason is that there are fewer children with their faces pressed against their nursery windows, chanting: 'Snow, snow faster! '

This morning, when I first caught sight of the unfamiliar whitened world, I could not help wishing that we had snow oftener, that English winters were more wintry. How delightful it would be, I thought, to have months of clean snow and a landscape sparkling with frost instead of innumerable grey featureless days of rain and raw winds. I began to envy my friends in such places as the eastern states of America and Canada, who can count upon a solid winter every year and know that the snow will arrive by a certain date and will remain, without degenerating into black slush, until spring is close at hand. To have snow and frost and yet a clear sunny sky and air as crisp as a biscuit – this seemed to me happiness indeed. And then I saw that it would never do for us. We should be sick of it in a week. After the first day, the magic would be gone and there would be nothing left but the unchanging glare of the day and the bitter cruel nights. It is not the snow itself, the sight of the blanketed world, that is so enchanting, but the first coming of the snow, the sudden and silent change. Out of the relations, for ever shifting and unanticipated, of wind and water comes a magical event. Who would change this state of things for a steadily recurring round, an earth governed by the calendar? It has been well said that while other countries have a climate, we alone in England have weather. There is nothing duller than climate, which can be converted into a topic only by scientists and hypochondriacs. But weather is our earth's Cleopatra, and it is not to be wondered at that we, who must share her gigantic moods, should be for ever talking about her. Once we were settled in America, Siberia, Australia, where there is nothing but a steady pact between climate and the calendar, we should regret her very naughtinesses, her wilful pranks, her gusts of rage and sudden tears. Waking in a morning would no longer be an adventure. Our weather may be fickle but it is no more fickle than we are, and only matches our inconstancy with her changes. Sun, wind, snow, rain, how welcome they are at first and how soon we grow weary of them! If this snow lasts a week, I shall be heartily sick of it and glad to speed its going. But its coming has been an event. Today has had a quality, an atmosphere, quite different from that of yesterday, and I have moved through it feeling a slightly different person, as if I were staying with new friends or had suddenly arrived in Norway. A man might easily spend five hundred pounds trying to break the crust of indifference in his mind, and yet feel less than I did this morning. Thus there is something to be said for leading the life of a Jane Austen character.

– Carless at Last –

1929

I suppose there are thousands of people in this country who are now telling themselves that they are happy because at last they have cars. But what is their happiness compared with mine? At odd moments throughout the day I remember that I have no car, and there is more music in my heart than ever came out of Daventry Experimental. Sometimes I forget that it has really gone for ever. I think of it being away in some garage, eating its head off; I imagine that I shall soon have to go once more and hear the lying reports of the mechanics; I take up my letters expecting to find among them those bills for repairs that are as crazy and vindictive as the proclamations of Oriental tyrants. And then I remember. It has gone for ever; there are no more garages, mechanics, bills for repair; I am no longer an owner-driver but a free man. There is an astonishing feeling of lightness and ease about the shoulders. No longer have I to support a huge and dubious piece of mechanism and its sneering and shrugging attendants in overalls. The thing may have made me look richer than I am, but it certainly made me feel miserably poor. Now that it has gone, I seem to be quite comfortably off again. I take trains and buses and taxis (without having to ask myself 'Why don't you use the car?') and I am amazed to find how cheap they are. It is a pleasure to travel now. It is also a pleasure to stay at home, for now there is no five-seater open tourer on the premises to remind me that I ought to be going somewhere in it in order to get my money's worth.

My mind to me a kingdom is. The R.A.C. and the A.A. are fading into meaningless initials. Double Shell is something in an ugly dream. I pass Dunlop and Michelin without so much as a nod. The Golden Pump is one of the innumerable blots on the landscape, nothing more. If any more young men don overalls and dirty their faces, they will not do it at my expense. I am indifferent to the real character of Ethyl. Four, six, eight, or twenty cylinders, it is all one to me now. What they do to the gallon is a question that leaves me shrugging, and at last I have enough spare cash to discover, if necessary, what I can do to the gallon. I can look at the countryside again like a man and not like a mere slave of the wheel. I can afford to dislike your long straight roads, to welcome the narrowest and most winding of lanes. I like to see trams in a town. The sight of cattle in the streets gives me pleasure again. I smile at old ladies who wander into the middle of the road and then decide to turn back. The cyclist seems to me an innocent creature, not without a certain quaint beauty. I have shed a whole foul tangle of contempt and envy. The people who sit in long shining pieces of mechanism no longer seem any better than the people who are packed into a tiny box on wheels. I raise no more hats to the Rolls or the Daimler: neither do I put out my tongue at the oldest Ford. In that daft world of wheels and smells I am Gallio himself. I am happy and free, careless and carless. It is as if my mind – the metaphor comes to me from some vague dream – had been decarbonized.

I was never at ease in that world. True, the first car I had was an unusually incompetent, if not downright malicious, vehicle. It was a very good argument for mass production, for it was of a make so rare that I never found anybody who had ever heard of it, and most people seemed to imagine that I had invented the name – and probably made the car. There was always one part of the mechanism that was not working, and towards the end hardly anything was working; I remember taking one visitor to the station in it when neither footbrake nor handbrake, clutch nor gears, were doing duty, and even the steering-wheel was all loose – we simply rolled down to the station. The only advantage the car had over ordinary cars was that it required virtually no feeding. I never remember giving it any oil, and it only asked for a mere drop of petrol. I suspect that it was not an internal-combustion engine at all, but a car on a new principle – years before its time – and really worked by will-power. Probably in a century or two there will be nothing but cars like that, which will simply be *thought* along the road. Unfortunately, my own will was not strong enough, though undoubtedly I worked miracles with it. Men in garages regarded me with wonder and awe after they had examined it, and I have no doubt the more intolerant of these mechanics would have had me burned as a wizard if I had stayed in the neighbourhood.

My second – and last – car was very different. It was the product of a very well-known firm, and it looked imposing enough. It worked in the ordinary way, and so long as various expensive operations were performed upon it from time to time, it continued to work. But instead of being an ascetic, it was a down-right glutton. Petrol it consumed as fast as it could, but oil was its passion. It demanded the most extravagant brands, and it could never have enough of them. It would hardly visit the station under a quart, and when we went touring in it you could have followed our route simply by observing the trail of empty oil drums. I could never afford to buy myself a book or a cigar or a bottle of wine when I had that car, for as soon as I had a spare pound or two it cried out for more oil. It was like entertaining for ever a drunkard who touched nothing but champagne. Imagine the relief at seeing him reel away at last, and you can form an idea of my present state of mind. I cannot pass a garage without jingling the shillings in my pocket and feeling comparatively rich.

That I am a bad driver I will cheerfully admit. I think the trouble about driving is that it requires just the wrong amount of attention − at least from me. It is not absolutely a full-time job, needing all your concentrated powers, but neither is it a thing you can do properly while thinking about something else. This was always my mistake: I would go on so merrily that after a time I would begin to think about other things, and when I did return to the matter in hand I was always a few seconds too late, I was too late at High Wycombe, when I bent the front axle; at Ealing when I hit the tram; at Northwood when I ran into the oldest Ford in the world (it belonged to a bill-poster and smashed my radiator); at Newport, that horrible November afternoon, when I cracked the electric standard and gathered round me all the people of Monmouth. When I was not too dreamy I was too impatient. Thick traffic exasperated me. My friend P. actually likes driving through thick traffic, and spends many a happy hour reversing in the most crowded London thoroughfares. Such a taste is incomprehensible to me. It is as if a man liked putting in a morning doing up the most awkwardly shaped objects into parcels, at the risk of being fined or maimed if they were not absolutely neat. My own experiences were so unpleasant that merely to be a passenger in a car that is being driven through a tangle of traffic makes me sweat; and in Paris I shut my eyes and offer up a prayer. It is not that I am afraid of being killed or of killing anybody else (I was never in danger of doing that even when I drove myself); it is simply the thought of that familiar and sickening crash, the crowd and the questions and the fuss, that appals me, remembering as I do my own adventures.

Now I am well out of it, a free man again. I suffer no inconvenience, for there is no longer any pleasure in motoring itself and there are trains and buses and taxis enough to take me wherever I want to go. No more taxes and garage fees and bills for petrol and oil. No more maddening conferences with mechanics who know no more about cars than I do, and no more staggering charges for repairs. No more worries about good roads and bad roads and trams and policemen. I can no longer drop you anywhere. You will have to drop me, and when I go, notice how jaunty my step, how lively the tune I whistle, all so carless and free.

– My Forchern –

1929

I saw the sign up a side-street: Madame Dash – Palmist. I decided at once to have my character, my destiny, unveiled.

The way led up a narrow flight of stairs, shared by a number of people such as Poppleworth & Sons, Surveyors, and J. G. Burton & Co., Inquiry Agents. At first I could not find Madame Dash. There was no door bearing her name. I went up three flights of stairs that were narrower and dustier at every turn, and I found and refound Poppleworth & Sons and J. G. Burton & Co., but no Madame Dash. I returned to the street and looked up at the windows. One of them was draped in lace curtains. There, I told myself – and J. G. Burton could not have done better – there is Madame Dash. I climbed the stairs again, discovered the door that seemed to be nearest to the lace curtains, knocked, and was asked to enter.

The room was very dim because the end nearest the window had been partitioned off. A head appeared round the curtain of the partition and said: 'D'you want a reading? Just wite a mowment, please.' So I sat down in the remains of a leather armchair and waited in the dim room, which was very stuffy and reeked of cheap incense. I examined its four vases of artificial flowers and its two prints, *The Star of Bethlehem* and *Westward Bound: with the Compliments of the Canadian Shipping Line.* I sat there not one minute but ten, during which time there was a continual whispering behind the partition. Then at last two subdued-looking middle-aged women, who, I will swear, kept little sweets and tobacco shops and had husbands who disappeared ten years ago, crept round the curtain, and I was invited to take their place near the window, with Madame.

There was nothing of the alluring or sinister sibyl about Madame, who was short, plump, middle-aged, with a round red face and eyeglasses drolly supported by a very snub little nose. She was wearing a black dress and a rather dirty grey woollen jersey without sleeves, and looked like the owner of a cheap seaside boarding-house who occasionally attended meetings of the local Theosophical Society in winter. She had, however, a pleasant open face, and out of hours, with another sympathetic middle-aged woman and a cup of tea or a bottle of stout by her side, no doubt she would prove to be a very genial companion. At the moment, however, she was earnestness itself. She faced me across a little table, gave me a crystal, told me to cover it with my hands and think about those affairs that I wished her to discuss. Then she looked at my left hand. 'Well, yes, of course,' she began. It was just as if we had been talking for hours. Her voice had plunged straight into an easy, intimate tone. A very clever opening, I thought it.

'Well, yes, of course,' she said, 'you've always been sensitive and reserved, and so of course you've been misunderstood. You've reelly an affectionate niture, but people don't think so. Thet's how it is with you. And you've lost fythe. You're one as can see through people. You know what's at the beck of their minds when they're talking to you, you know if they're lying, if they're guilty or not. But being sow reserved, it's got you misunderstood a good deal, it has. And then you've lost your fythe. You follow me, downcher?'

This, extended afterwards to 'You follow me now, downcher?' was her favourite phrase, and sometimes she put it in sadly, sometimes it came out briskly, sometimes it arrived with a triumphant ring. What she would do without it, I cannot imagine, for it served all manner of purposes. It kept me nodding like a mandarin. So far I agreed with everything she said. Her view of my character was singularly like my own.

It was now the turn of my right hand. 'Yes,' she said, 'you've had to work hard, but up to now you've not had all you've been entitled to have from your work. Other people been getting the benefit. You follow me, downcher? People have picked your brains before to-day. Professional, aren't you? It's written here in your hand that you're professional. You'll do better this year than you've ever done before. The months of My and June'll be good for you, specially good. You'll arrive at a position of great responsibility, you will, before long. Up to know, though you might have done fairly well, you reelly haven't had your chance. You follow me, downcher?'

Yes, I was following her. All these were, emphatically, my sentiments. At the moment I could not think of the names of the rascals who had been picking my brains and stealing the fruits of my endeavour, but I had no doubt at all that they existed.

'And another thing,' Madame pursued. 'Anybody looking at you would think you were a gentleman who had the best of health, but you haven't, you know, reelly. You've not been as well as you might have been since last November, nothing like so well as you look. You see what I mean?'

I agreed with enthusiasm. It is perfectly true that I am hardly ever as well as I look, and I have the misfortune to be surrounded by people – relatives, friends, and even doctors – who simply cannot understand this, who do not realize what I suffer in my own quietude.

She had finished with my hands now, and began gazing into the crystal I had been holding. 'I see a Nightch,' she announced, impressively. 'A Nightch!' I cried, startled. 'Yes, the letter Ightch,' she said. 'D'you know anybody whose nime begins with a Nightch?' But this did not take us far because I know so many people whose names begin with that letter. She mentioned several other initial letters too, but this was easily the least valuable part of the séance. I refused to take an interest in these vague alphabetical creatures.

'I see money coming to you from two directions,'

she said, peering in the crystal. 'It's in here, two different directions. Can you understand what that means?
It's money coming to you soon.' I am accustomed to
seeing money depart in all directions, but the thought
of it coming, two shining streams converging upon me,
was new and distinctly pleasant. I did not understand
what it meant (or if I did, I do not see why I should tell
everybody), but for a moment I enjoyed the thrill of
one about to be rich.

'I see a tall gentleman, very straight he is – he
stands up in here – oldish gentleman, and he means
well to you. You can trust him. And there's a younger
gentleman, dark with a thin fice, and he's to be trusted
too. And these two'll bring you in a lot of money. And
you're doing a lot of signing, a lot of signing. You follow
me, downcher?' 'Well,' I said, hesitantly, 'as a matter of
fact, I always have a good deal of signing to do.' 'But
we don't see here anything you do in the ordinary way
of things,' she said. 'This is special signing, something
that'll please you.' She stared again in silence for a few
moments. 'You're in a city with narrow streets and very
tall buildings, you've had to go there on business, and
it's very lucky for you. Very narrow streets and very tall
buildings. Liverpool or Manchester, p'raps.'

'I hope not,' I murmured. It is one thing to be told
you are to be lucky in some strange city, and it is quite
another thing to be told you will be in Liverpool or
Manchester. I felt disappointed, but clung to the hope
that topography was not her strong point.

Her next remark was rather reassuring. 'The streets mayn't be so narrow,' she observed, 'because it may be only the buildings that are so high. Anyhow I see you there, and it'll be lucky for you.' Which left me with a conviction that the city was New York, that I was to be there signing contracts for plays, films, serial stories, short stories, five-hundred-dollar articles on The American Woman as I See Her, with men straight as ramrods standing by, looking after my interests. 'Now, you can ask me anything you like,' she said, but really by this time I felt there was little to ask. After a minute or two, during which she told me again that I was reserved, sensitive, affectionate, misunderstood, witty and keen-brained, unlucky so far but about to be very successful, and that all I wanted was a little fythe, I did put a question, but it was only to ask her what I owed her. 'It's half a crown, that is, if you're satisfied,' she replied.

Satisfied! I should think I was. Without knowing my age or profession, anything of my personal history, she had yet contrived to tell me all the things that I want to be told, the things I have always secretly believed to be true of myself and that nobody but me – and this kindly oracle – ever seemed to understand. The session was worth a hundred half-crowns. It was a daydream of oneself suddenly conjured into an oracular utterance. It was a visit to a magic mirror.

As I went out, I saw two people waiting their turn. I only had a glimpse of them, but it was enough to show

me that they too would prove to be reserved, affectionate, sensitive, misunderstood, unfortunate perhaps
up to now but about to rush into prosperity, immense
good fortune. I thought of them pleasantly as I passed
the doors of Poppleworth & Sons, Surveyors, and J. G.
Burton & Co., Inquiry Agents, and descended into the
world again.

– Dissolution in Haymarket –

1932

S urely there is hardly a street in London less
morbid, more determined in its own sedate fashion to make something out of life, than Haymarket.
Indeed, now I come to think of it, Haymarket is one
of my favourite thoroughfares. It has a pleasant gen-
tlemanly air, with just a suggestion of the eighteenth
century, and has, too, all manner of interesting things
in it. To begin with, there are its two large theatres,
one of which is associated in my mind with a number
of charming plays, and the other – I regret to say – only
with camels. There are the Stores and a fine old tobacco shop, and, best of all, the shipping agents with their
model steamers and little panoramas. Those steamers
alone – and there are quite a number of them – lift the
whole street high above the common level. The sight
of them prevents London from closing in on you, for
it suddenly opens some little windows in what seems
the grey wall of the street, and through these windows
come flashing the bright dunes and red roofs of Denmark or the shining peaks of the Sierra Nevada. If this
is not enough, flanking them you have the actual windows of the little panoramas, which artfully combine
in themselves the lure of travel and the excitement of

a toy theatre. No, it would be hard to find a London street less morbid, less gloomy, more likely to augment rather than diminish one's zest for life.

Yet as I was journeying on a bus down Haymarket the other day, about the lunch hour, there suddenly came crashing down upon me a mood such as I have never known before. It was as if a huge black stone had been flung into the pool of my consciousness. It all happened (as we were told it would) in the twinkling of an eye. Everything was changed. The whole cheerful pageant of the street immediately crumpled and collapsed, with all its wavering pattern of light and shade, its heartening sights and sounds, its warm humanity, its suggestion of permanence, and I was left shivering in the middle of a tragedy. Not something magnificent, you understand, with funereal guns roaring out over the battlements of Elsinore or queens with bright hair dying for love, nothing after the high Roman fashion; but a dreary tragedy of cheated fools and illusions blown to the winds, of withering and decay, dust and worms. I saw this world for a moment or so through the hollow eyes of the prophets and the great pessimists, and what I saw left me shivering with cold and sick at heart. Nor did there remain with me that cosy painted chamber of the mind into which I might retire, there to forget in comfort, for it, too, was desolated, heaped about with cold ashes and with its tattered curtains flapping in the wind. All the stir and noise and glitter seemed nothing but fast-shredding pigment on a dead face.

I might have been old Donne himself, brooding over corruption and putrefaction and the gnawing worm; and it was his words that returned to me: '. . . all our life is but a going out to the place of execution, to death'. What was the bus I was in but a greasy tumbril, and what were all of us, jogging there empty-eyed, littered with our foolish paraphernalia of newspapers, umbrellas, parcels, but a company of the doomed? There we were, so many grinning skeletons masquerading in this brief and bitter carnival as fat citizens, charwomen, bus conductors, chorus girls; idly juggling with thoughts of our destinations, the offices, restaurants, clubs, theatres that claimed us; when, in truth, we had all but one sure destination – perhaps round the next corner – the narrow grave. 'The sun is setting to thee, and that for ever.' And on the face of everyone there, hurrying with me to the place of execution, I read the marks of weakness and decay, and seemed to see that untiring hand at work furrowing the brow and dimming the eyes. Everywhere was dissolution. The whole street was mouldering and rotting, hastening with all that was in it to its inevitable end. The crowds I saw through the windows seemed made up of creatures that were either gross or wasted, shuffling, bent, twisted in limb, already bleached and mangled by disease; and here and there among the crowd, in bright contrast and yet infinitely more pitiful, were the few who had youth and strength and beauty, who moved as if they thought they could live for ever – who had not yet heard, from afar, the hammering, the slow tread, the pattering of earth upon the coffin.

There was something more than the old thought, death is certain, festering in the heart of that mood. That, indeed, is a thought we are always quite willing to salute, with a mere wave of the hand, but are really very unready to entertain, except when we make its first acquaintance in childhood, when it has a trick of bringing a whole host of grimacing shadows about our besides. But there was something more behind that sudden tragic vision I had. There was a sense of universal dissolution, of this life as a pitiful piece of cheating, of bright promise all ruthlessly scattered. Nothing remained but the certainty of decay and death. The more you loved life, delighting in whatever it had of beauty and goodness to offer you, the more openly you bared your breast for the stroke of its dagger. I saw all of us there – my fellow-passengers in the bus, the driver and the conductor, the policeman and the hawkers, the playgoers waiting at the pit door, the crowds shopping or loafing – as the victims of this great treachery, lured into worshipping a loveliness that must fade and pass, trapped into setting our hearts upon things we can never keep with us, upon beings who smile for an hour and then miserably perish. It is well, I thought, for the grandest of our old preachers to say: 'We long for perishing meat, and fill our stomachs with corruption; we look after white and red, and the weaker beauties of the night; we are passionate after rings and seals, and enraged at the breaking of a crystal', and then to make it plain that these things will not avail us. But other and nobler things, it seemed to me, would avail us even less, for the more we opened our hearts, making ourselves eager and loving, the more certain amid this universal dissolution was our ultimate misery. We are the poor playthings of Time, dandled for an hour and then flung to rot in a corner; and yet we are all born, as was said of Coleridge, hungering for Eternity.

So brimmed with such thoughts, feelings, old quotations, strange images, clustering together like the pieces in a kaleidoscope to form one tragic vision of things, I was carried down the desolated length of Haymarket, where man spendeth his vain life as a shadow. As those last words will suggest, my mood had by that time crystallized into the utter hopelessness of that other and great Preacher. Vanity of vanities! Had I been a natural man instead of the smooth mountebank demanded by decency and encouraged by my natural timidity, I should have descended from the bus, put ashes on my head, and cried 'Woe!' to the assembled hawkers and playgoers and policemen, stunning them with gigantic metaphors. That is what, in my heart, I wanted to do, so surely was I possessed by this sudden hopeless vision and by a mixed feeling of contempt and pity for my fellow mortals. Yet I sat there, quietly enough, and still well aware of the fact that I was on my way to lunch with two friends at a club not very far away. I was, as it were, purely automatically aware of this fact, for in those last moments, so rapt had I been in my vision, I had no sense even of personal identity. But I moved forward, as a man might over a darkening field of battle, towards the club and my friends, and arrived there and greeted them in a kind of dream; and then, suddenly, out of my dream, I looked at them sharply and curiously, these friends of mine, whose grim sentence and that of all they held dear still seemed to be ringing in my ears. How strangely childish, touchingly naive, their smiling confidence, their little preoccupations, their chatter. I saw them seating themselves opposite me at the lunch table, and it was as if they were people acting on a distant stage; yet I did not feel completely detached from them, but, on the contrary, felt a kind of tenderness for them and all their little toys and antics. Then I heard one of these doomed creatures propose that we should drink Burgundy. I stood out for something lighter, for though I like a glass of Burgundy as well as the next man, I maintain it is far too heavy for lunch.

– On the Moors –

1932

If you go from Bradford to Bingley, from Bingley to Eldwick, then up the hill from Eldwick, you arrive at Dick Hudson's. Mr Hudson will not be there to greet you, because he has been dead this long time. But the old grey inn that stands on the edge of the moors is called by his name and by no other. Even the little bus that runs up there now has 'Dick Hudson's' boldly painted on its signboard. And there's a pleasant little immortality for you. 'We'll go,' they say to one another in Bradford, and have said as long as I can remember – 'we'll go as far as Dick Hudson's.' If you start from the other end, climbing the moorland track from Ilkley, you will inevitably come to Dick Hudson's when you finally drop down from the high moor, and if the hour is right, you will inevitably have a pint of bitter at Dick's. That is what I did, the other day. I returned, after years of southern exile, to the moors, and began by having two pints at Dick's. And I was mightily relieved to find it still there, the same old grey building, the same cool interior, still smelling of good beer and fried ham; for at any moment now, they may begin monkeying with the old place, turning it into an ice-cream parlour or some such horror.

If you live in Bradford, Shipley, Keighley, you kindle at the sound of Dick Hudson's. That is not merely because you have been so often refreshed there, but chiefly because you know it is the most familiar gateway to the moors. The moors to the West Riding folk are something more than a picnic place, a pretty bit of local country-side. They are the grand escape. In the West Riding towns you have something to escape from, for industrial mankind has done its worst there. But the moors are always waiting for you, and you have only to leave the towns for an hour or two, climbing the hills, to see them dwindle into a vague smoulder and a sheen of glass roofs in the valleys, then vanish, and perhaps be forgotten. The moors are there, miles and miles of country-side that has not changed for centuries, and you have only to squeeze through the little hole in the wall, just beyond Dick Hudson's to take your fill of them. It does not matter who you are, for they are yours while you are there, and the richest wool man in the town can claim no more right in them than you can. Once through that hole in the wall, you have escaped miraculously; and if you were a favoured lad in a fairy tale you could have no better luck, no more elaborate transformation worked for you, for one afternoon. So if you are a stranger to those parts and should visit them, do not let the black streets, the monotonous rows of little houses almost set on end, the trams that drone away between factories, the whole grim paraphernalia of old-fashioned industrialism, depress you too much, but please remember that the winds that suddenly swoop down on the sooty slates have come over leagues of moorland and still have the queer salty tang in them.

Well, I had my pints at Dick Hudson's, went through the little hole in the wall, and climbed on to the moor, as I had so many times before and yet had not done for many a year. It was a weekday and very quiet. The sun was hot and seemed to smite these uplands, bruising every blade and blossom so that they sent out sharp odours. Once more I seemed to be walking on the roof of England. The singing larks only rose a little way from the ground, as if they were high enough now. The winds came sliding or shooting over the top, at no more than shoulder height, and there was in them the old magical scent, earthy enough and yet with always something of the sea in it, that strange saltiness. Against the brown hillsides I saw the tender green of the young bracken. There, once more, were the tumbled rocks, floating in and out of the great cloud shadows; the ruined byres and the mysterious stone walls; the granite dust of the moorland path glittering in the sunlight. I heard again the baa-ing of the moorland sheep, like complaining voices coming from great hollows. Everything there was as it had always been.

Down in the valleys, among the streets I once knew so well, they were putting up new buildings and tearing down old ones, they were going into bankruptcy or starting afresh, old men were dying and young men were marrying, and nothing was standing still. The life of the town was hurrying away from the life that I once knew, and down there, among the stalwarts that had so suddenly and strangely grown bent, grey and old, and the babies that had so suddenly and strangely shot up into young men and women, I was rapidly becoming a man from another place, a stranger. But up there, on the moors, there were no changes at all. I saw what I had always seen, and there was no sense that did not receive the same old benediction.

Yet it was not the same. I sat down on the smooth springy grass, with my back against a rock, and as I smoked my pipe in that high lonely place, I tried to disentangle it all. I was happy to be there again, and not a sight, a sound, an odour, that returned to me failed to give me pleasure, and yet in this happiness there was the strangest melancholy. It was as if there was between me and these dear and familiar sights and sounds a sheet of glass. I felt as if I had only to pluck the ling and heather at my side for it to wither and crumble in my hand. I might have been a man on parole for one golden afternoon from some distant internment camp. There were no tears in my eyes but I will swear my mind knew the salt glitter of them. If I had spoken to a fellow-traveller then, he would have concluded that I was a man who had once known great happiness in these parts and had then gone into some sad exile. And he would have been wrong. I am happier now than ever I was when I used to come to these moors week in and week out, when I was on the easiest and friendliest terms with them, and every rock and clump of heather spoke to me in my own language. When I walked these moors then, or stretched myself on the grassy carpet in the sun, hour after hour, I spent my time dreaming of the happiness that would be mine when I should be as I actually am now. I do not say that I was really unhappy in those days, for I was a healthy youngster with plenty of things to do and with many good friends, but I was certainly restless and dissatisfied and apt to be sulkily despondent in a world that did not appear to appreciate my unique merit. I thought I was a fine fellow then, but nevertheless I had not acquired that armour of conceit which begins to protect our self-esteem later in life, that armour which compels some elderly members of my profession to move so ponderously. I could be snubbed then, could retire in haste, all hot and pricking, from many a company. There is no doubt whatever that I am happier now.

What hocus-pocus, what sentimental attitudinizing, was it then that made me feel so melancholy, the other afternoon on the moors? I was not an exile at all. If I want to live near the moors and visit them every day, there is nothing to prevent me. I could go there, and stay there, tomorrow, if I really wanted to. I know very well that I don't want to, that I would much rather live where I do live. I am well aware of the fact that the moors would bore me very soon and that I get more out of them by visiting them now and again than I ever would by living near them. Like most people, I have lost several persons very dear to me, but, there again, to be honest, I must confess that there is nobody who is associated with the moors in my mind who is now lost to me. The only possible person is that other, younger self, who had trod these very paths so often; but then, I do not mourn him. Let the young cub perish. First youth has gone, it is true, but I do not see that there is anything specially admirable in early youth. I have strength and vigour, a sense of fun and a sense of wonder, still with me, and I have not the slightest desire to be nineteen again. All this I pointed out to myself, as I sat against that rock and watched the great purple cloud shadows drift across the moorland, but that feeling of melancholy remained and would not budge. It was like one horn, amid the happy tumult of a full orchestra, ceaselessly sounding a little theme of despair. If the moors were real, then I was a ghost. If I was real, then all his sober richness of bracken and heather and tumbled rock and blue sky was a mirage, a bubble landscape that one determined forefinger could prick so that it gave a wink and then vanished for ever. I returned, a man in a puzzling dream, but also a hot and thirsty man, to Dick Hudson's.

– Strange Encounter –

1932

Yesterday, the people in the bungalow below took us to Hartland in their car. We went through Stratton, whose oldest inn has a notice that reminds you that the battle of Stamford Hill was fought just round the corner. And there are such perils, such hairbreadth escapes, in Stratton's narrow and twisting street, where gigantic buses miss you by an inch, that all the battles of that Civil War seem part of an idyll, old and happy, far-off things. We went, through Kilk-hampton, where I saw nothing of interest except one of those queer families, those monstrous collections of odd humans, that you never see except when you are travelling. It is impossible to imagine them at home. We climbed to the top of a rustling moor, and then crossed it in happy solitude. We ran down steep and narrow lanes, and at last came to the headland where there is a crazy hotel and the ruins of Hartland Quay. A green sea shook itself now and again and then went creaming over the rocks. It was far below the shattered brickwork of the old quay, but you felt it was giving a glance in that direction every now and then, and mut-tering, 'Just try building another breakwater, that's all! Just try it!' Lundy, that familiar speck, was now a big fat rock of an island, almost absurdly melodramatic. I spent a dreamy half-hour – and every scribbler will know how pleasant it was – vaguely planning a thriller that would have a Lundy chapter or two in it. The others, I believe, were trying to decide whether the blackbird fluttering about the face of the cliff really was a raven. Perhaps it was, as we shall see, and was trying to cry 'nevermore'.

We walked to the top of the cliff, and watched some great buzzard hawks go wheeling up into the blue. There were sweet smells, an old intoxication, in the air. To have the heather about your feet and to look out to sea is to be happy, so happy that you feel it is incredible that you will not live for ever. But the shadow of mortality soon fell upon us. We arrived at Stoke Church. This church is miles from anywhere, except from the rocks and foam and the ruined quay, the gulls and ravens and hawks, yet it lifts a great tower to the sky, just as if the bustling plains of Flanders were beneath it. There are a few white-washed cottages, a few gnarled trees, and this church with its enormous tower. We wandered about the churchyard, in which a whole host has been buried, so that mounds and stones almost jostle one another. There you may meet generations of Chopes and Prusts and Okes, whole centuries of them. Their stones show a grim appreciation of the fact of death. Our ancestors may have had their weaknesses, but sentimentality about death was not one of them. They lived round the churchyard. Not a single passing coffin escaped their eyes. When they died themselves, they pointed out, in clear inch lettering in granite, that you would soon be dead too. The Shropshire Lad himself had not a better eye for all the signs of mortality, but they did not make the same fuss about it. Here was the older Western Front and all was quiet upon it, but decency and reticence had been given a turn too. In the lovely old interior of the church was a tablet to a local gentleman, and he was described, simply and superbly, as 'a plain good man'. I do not think that I am a plain good man, but I felt that here was a community in which I could have lived without frequently suspecting that we were all mad together.

And it was here, in this remote western corner, this place of foam and heather and great wild birds, among the unknown Chopes and Okes and Prusts, that I discovered my old publisher – John Lane. He lies in this very churchyard, and in the church itself there is a memorial tablet to him. It was the queerest, the most startling encounter. I knew that he came from some little place in Devonshire, but I had forgotten – if I ever knew – that it was Hartland, and that he was buried in Stoke Church. I stared and stared at his name. The memory of the man himself returned to me, very vividly. I only knew him during his last years. He was my first London publisher, and for several years I was his 'reader'. He used to give me lunch at his clubs, the Reform and the Cocoa Tree, and dinner down at Lancaster Gate. I saw again his short figure, his bearded face, his peering vague eyes. I heard again his curiously characteristic tones, at once a little hoarse and squeaky. It seemed only a month or two ago since we were sitting in some corner, heavy with cigar smoke, and I was listening to his rambling good talk about some portrait he had picked up or the idiosyncrasies of one of his older poets. He was one of those men – and I mean only the men with whom one has business relations – of whom it might be said that they cannot be approved of or recommended and yet cannot be disliked. He was one of the old school of publishers, a sort of genial literary brigand, who believed quite sincerely that authors should not have any money, and so whittled down your terms to nearly nothing, but at the same time poured champagne and liqueur brandy down your throat and pressed upon you the largest cigars. He would give you anything so long as it was not a matter of percentages. The idea of an author who had an agent and a decent bank account and artful notions about dramatic rights shocked him. Authors to him were either people in society with incomes or wild geniuses who simply needed a good lunch or dinner now and again to keep them going. He always seemed to know about books, though I can never believe he ever read any. He was a character, and I liked him enormously.

Devon boys have roamed about these heathery Hartland cliffs, gone out into the world and, after many Odysseys, have returned to this remote place to die. But few of them, for all the epics of Moorish galleys, sacked towns, and sunken gold, can have had a queerer history than this of John Lane. Only the day before I had been reading an advance copy of Miss Viola Meynell's delightful life of her mother, Alice Meynell, and John Lane had popped up there. He pops up everywhere in the Nineties. He was himself an intensely respectable man, a solid bourgeois, but as a publisher he had a flair and knew when the moment had arrived for naughtiness and fine writing and devil take the suburbs. As I strolled away from that churchyard, where cavalier's man, eighteenth-century farmhand, and Victorian coastguard all lie so peacefully together, and their times seem all one under that wide gull-haunted sky, I thought about the queer adventures of this wandering Devonian. How far away, how odd, seemed all the old activities of that Bodley Head! The 'nest of singing birds'. The 'decadents'. Beardsley and Harland and the Yellow Book. 'I have been true to thee, Cynara, in my fashion.' John Davidson, with his ballads and eclogues. Max Beerbohm's *Works*. Le Gallienne's *Quest of the Golden Girl*. The *Keynotes* Series. And the little man with the peaked beard and the near-sighted eyes threaded his way through these things, smoked his cigar at the Reform and the Cocoa Tree, surveyed his first editions and portraits at Lancaster Gate, conjured Anatole France into yellow-coloured English volumes, and then left what was mortal of him under the shadow of these Hartland Cliffs.

– Different Inside –

1932

I have been misunderstood and wrongly accused so many times that I ought to be able now to shrug my shoulders, not merely suffering in silence (for I know that protest is useless) but being indifferent, not suffering at all. Yet every other day or so something happens and I see once more what an ill-fated fellow I am. Only last night, for example, when we were playing bridge at my cousin's, she accused me of being far too pleased with myself when I contrived (not unskilfully, let me admit) to be four up in spades. The fact is, of course, that she was still rather annoyed because she had for once been overcalled, she who calls so wildly and unscrupulously and always forgets to pay, or at least forgets to pay me, when she loses. That is not the point, however, and I have no intention of discussing my cousin's fantastic ethics. The trouble is that I know very well she had evidence enough on which to base her accusation. No doubt my face was one vast ill-mannered grin of triumph, a revolting sight, and yet I was not feeling jubilant, ready to crow at my victory, but only mildly pleased with myself. I did not even know I was looking pleased, having forgotten for the moment the tricks my face plays on me. I can well believe, however, that I presented to the company a front that irritated everybody. Are other people, I wonder, as plagued by their faces as I am by mine, which thus monstrously exaggerates and distorts every feeling it is called upon to express; or do I suffer alone – a man with a calm philosophic mind but with a face that long ago decided to go on the stage, and the melodramatic stage at that, a man with his heart in the right place but with his features in Hollywood?

When I first entered adult life I imagined, like the young idiot I then was, that I had complete control of my face. I was convinced that I could permit myself to feel anything behind that bland disguise. When I went out for the evening and found myself becoming more and more bored by the company, I was sure that nobody but myself was aware of the fact. I set my face, as best I could from behind, to register a polite or even eager interest; I put on a smile and kept it there, left my eyes to sparkle away, and so forth; and then felt, even though the smile seemed rather stiff towards the end of the evening, that I could relapse with safety into comfortable boredom. As I never saw myself, it was some time before I was disillusioned. We never lose any of our illusions about ourselves in the company of strangers. But I made friends, and in this, as in other matters, they very quickly disillusioned me as they strolled, in the usual friendly fashion, through the house of my mind and casually opened a few windows here and there to let in the east wind. One would say:

'Dullish at the So-and-so's the other night, I thought. You looked dreadfully bored.' A succession of such remarks soon revealed to me the true state of things, and I realized that I had been deceiving myself. It was not for me to try to look one thing when I was thinking and feeling another. The idea of myself as one of your smooth fellows, made for diplomacy and the best society, for ever charming yet secretly tired of it all, would no longer hold, and, bearing in mind my newer and truer relations with my face, I was compelled to revise my estimate of myself.

There was, however, nothing alarming or even really disappointing in the situation. I was not sorry to be free from the strain of a diplomatic bearing, and congratulated myself on the fact that the higher types of human beings do not wear a smooth and impassive front. There is nothing better than an open, honest countenance, frankly expressing to the world its owner's feelings. I thought so then and I think so still, though now my opinion is worth more if only because it is more disinterested. I imagined then that mine was one of those open, honest faces, and was happy in this belief until the cumulative effect of a series of misunderstandings, of which that one last night is a good example, compelled me to take stock of myself once more, with the result that I was disillusioned once and for all. I found that people were always telling me not to be so angry when, in actual fact, I was only slightly annoyed, were for ever asking me why I was so jubilant when in truth I was only mildly pleased, were constantly suggesting that I should not glare furiously at strangers when I was only conscious of feeling a little curious. At last I realized the truth. My face did not even honestly reflect my mind but grossly caricatured it. I was carrying into all companies a monstrous libel of myself. It was as if I were compelled to wear a set of features that did not belong to me at all but to some other and very different kind of man. Small wonder, then, that I should be so frequently misjudged, for it is not unnatural that people should imagine that these facial antics, for which I am held responsible though they seem to be entirely beyond my control, are an indication of my state of mind. How are they to know that my face has apparently an independent existence, setting to work merely on a hint from my mind and then going on in a fashion of which I strongly disapprove.

That is the irony of the situation. My face would seem to belong to a type of man I dislike. It is a theatrical, temperamental affair, for ever rushing out to extremes, whereas I am all for moderation. I do not pretend to absolute philosophic calm and detachment, but – whatever my acquaintances, the deluded audience of this face, may say to the contrary – I am certainly not a man of strong feelings, one of those people who must be excited about something, who are not happy unless they are in the depths of misery or find all existence wretched because they do not feel ecstatic, who must be always yearning and burning, loving and hating, laughing and crying. Not only have I a contempt for such persons, but I could not imitate them if I would. Such emotions as I have are small and safe and never likely to get out of hand. Ecstasy and despair do not come my way and are never likely to be encountered in the easy rambles that my mind takes every day. My attitude towards my fellow-creatures is one of timid goodwill, tempered here by tranquil affection and there by a faint hostility. Even the kind of man who ought, at this moment, to be wearing my face only arouses a dislike that stops very far short of definite hatred. When, let us say (for last night still rankles), I win a game, I am only conscious of feeling a slight pleasure, spiced by just the slightest sense of triumph; and when I lose, as I do very frequently, I am certain that I am visited by nothing stronger than a tiny feeling of disappointment, a mere mental sigh. I have been guilty, in my time, of some meanness and may have contrived, here and there, to do a kindness, but never yet have I played either the villain or the hero. If life is a melodrama – and sometimes it has every appearance of being one – then I am certainly a very minor character. In short, I am a well fed, comfortable, calm and not entirely unphilosophical adult male, with no desire for raging emotions and with precious few to rage.

That is what I am really like inside. Outside, apparently, everything is different, thanks to a set of features that totally misrepresent me. So far as I can gather, my face pounces on the least whisper in my mind, as it were, and transforms it into a shout. It grins insolently and sickeningly with triumph over a mere hand at cards. It scowls ferociously at inoffensive strangers, screams 'You're a bore!' at prattling callers, and twists and writhes, lights up or fades out, falls into a sodden mass of depression, glitters with mischief, gapes or grins or glares, at every fresh turn the conversation takes. It transforms every hour into a benefit performance by a bad actor of the old school, strutting and mouthing insanely in the limelight. A talking ape with a megaphone could not produce a worse caricature of its master. While the company I am in is staring at this monstrous show, I sit there innocently behind it all, an unassuming fellow with nothing but a pleasant little rise and fall of emotion, entirely forgetting that this awful travesty of my mind is taking place until some strange misunderstanding bids me remember how grotesquely and unhappily I am situated. Am I alone in my trouble or has there been a general misdeal of faces? Perhaps there are other unfortunates for whom the situation has been reversed, who find themselves possessed of the most towering emotions, yet cannot make their passion felt because their faces refuse to express anything beyond a slight feeling of annoyance or a tranquil pleasure. If there are any such persons, I should like to meet one of them for the purpose of comparing our baffled sensations and of finally forming and consolidating a friendship. We could at least enjoy one another's faces.

– The Reunion Battalion Dinner –

from *English Journey*, 1934

I had arranged to meet, in a little ante-room, the survivors of my original platoon, and as soon as I decently could I escaped from the press of warriors in the big room, to revisit my own past. There were about eight of us present, and we ordered in some drinks and settled down to remember aloud. I had not seen any of these fellows for seventeen years. I knew them all, of course, and they seemed little older. The difference was that before they had all been soldiers, whereas now their respective status in civilian life set its mark upon them, and now one was a clerk, another a tram-conductor, another a mill-hand, and so forth. Nearly all of them remembered more than I did, although I have an exceptionally good memory. Details that had vanished for ever from my mind were easily present to theirs. Why? Was it because a defensive mechanism in my mind had obliterated as much as it could from my memory; or was it because much more had happened to me since the war than had happened to them and, unlike them, I had not gone back over and over again to those war years? (A third explanation, of course, is that, living in the same district and often running across one another, they had talked over those years far more than I had.) As figure after figure, comic and tragic, came looming through the fog of years, as place after place we had been in caught the light again, our talk became more and more eager and louder, until we shouted and laughed in triumph, as one always does when Time seems to be suffering a temporary defeat. Frensham, Aldershot, Folkestone, Maidstone, Bully Grenay, Neuve Chapelle, Souchez – how they returned to us! Once again the water was rising round our gum boots. We remembered the fantastic places: that trench which ran in front of a graveyard, where the machine-gun bullets used to ricochet off the tombstones; that first sight of Vimy Ridge in the snow, like a mountain of despair. We recalled to one another the strange co-incidences and dark premonitions: poor melancholy B. who muttered, 'I'll be lying out there to-night,' and was, a dead man that very night; grim Sergeant W. who said to the draft, 'This is where you can expect to have your head blown off,' and had his own head shattered by a rifle-grenade within three hours. And little Paddy O., who had always seemed such a wisp of a chap, with everything about him drooping, who looked the same as ever, ready to drop at any moment, though he never had dropped and the Central Powers must have spent hundreds of thousands of marks trying to kill him, little Paddy, I say, came close to me, finished his beer, and asked me, stammeringly as ever, if I remembered sending him from the front line for some water for the platoon, on a summer morning in 1916. 'Nay,' he stammered, 'I wasn't gone more than t-ten minutes, and when I c-come back, where you'd been, Jack lad, there was n-nobbut a bloody big hole and I n-never set eyes on you again till to-night.' And it was true. I had sent him away on a ten minutes' errand; immediately afterwards a giant trench mortar had exploded in the very entrance to the little dug-out where I was dividing up the platoon rations; I had been rushed away, and was gone before he returned; and it had taken us more than seventeen years to find one another again.

Several of us had arranged with the secretary to see that the original members of the battalion to whom the price of the dinner was prohibitive were provided with free tickets. But this, he told me, had not worked very well; and my old platoon comrades confirmed this, too, when I asked about one or two men. They were so poor, these fellows, that they said they could not attend the dinner even if provided with free tickets because they felt that their clothes were not good enough. They ought to have known that they would have been welcome in the sorriest rags; but their pride would not allow them to come. (It was not a question of evening clothes; this dinner was largely for ordinary working men.) I did not like to think then how bad their clothes, their whole circumstances, were: it is not, indeed, a pleasant subject. They were with us, swinging along while the women and old men cheered, in that early battalion of Kitchener's New Army, were with us when kings, statesmen, general officers, all reviewed us, when the crowds threw flowers, blessed us, cried over us; and then they stood in the mud and water, scrambled through the broken strands of barbed wire, saw the sky darken and the earth open with red-hot steel, and came back as official heroes and also as young-old workmen wanting to pick up their jobs and their ordinary life again; and now, in 1933, they could not even join us in a tavern because they had not decent coats to their backs. We could drink to the tragedy of the dead; but we could only stare at one another, in pitiful embarrassment, over this tragi-comedy of the living, who had fought for a world that did not want them, who had come back to exchange their uniforms for rags. And who shall restore to them the years that the locust hath eaten?

– from *Postscripts* –

I wonder how many of you feel as I do about this great Battle and evacuation of Dunkirk. The news of it came as a series of surprises and shocks, followed by equally astonishing new waves of hope. It was all, from beginning to end, unexpected. And yet now that it's over, and we can look back on it, doesn't it seem to you to have an inevitable air about it – as if we had turned a page in the history of Britain and seen a chapter headed 'Dunkirk' – and perhaps seen too a picture of the troops on the beach waiting to embark?

And now that this whole action is completed, we notice that it has a definite shape, and a certain definite character. What strikes me about it is how typically English it is. Nothing, I feel, could be more English than this Battle of Dunkirk, both in its beginning and its end, its folly and its grandeur. It was very English in what was sadly wrong with it; this much has been freely admitted, and we are assured will be freely discussed when the proper moment arrives. We have gone sadly wrong like this before; and here and now we must re-solve never, never to do it again. Another such blunder may not be forgiven us.

But having admitted this much, let's do ourselves

the justice of admitting too that this Dunkirk affair was also very English (and when I say 'English' I really mean British) in the way in which, when apparently all was lost, so much was gloriously retrieved. Bright honour was almost 'plucked from the moon'. What began as a miserable blunder, a catalogue of misfortunes and miscalculations, ended as an epic of gallantry. We have a queer habit – and you can see it running through our history – of conjuring up such transformations. Out of a black gulf of humiliation and despair, rises a sun of blazing glory.

This is not the German way. They don't make such mistakes (a given fact that we should bear in mind) but also they don't achieve such epics. There is never anything to inspire a man either in their victories or in their defeats; boastful when they're winning, quick to whine when threatened with defeat – there is nothing about them that ever catches the world's imagination. That vast machine of theirs can't create a glimmer of that poetry of action which distinguishes war from mass murder. It's a machine – and therefore has no soul.

But here at Dunkirk is another English epic. And to my mind what was most characteristically English about it – so typical of us, so absurd and yet so grand and gallant that you hardly know whether to laugh or to cry when you read about them – was the part played in the difficult and dangerous embarkation – not by the warships, magnificent though they were – but by the little pleasure-steamers. We've known them and laughed at them, these fussy little steamers, all our lives. We have called them 'the shilling sticks.' We have watched them load and unload their crowds of holiday passengers – the gents full of high spirits and bottled beer, the ladies eating pork pies, the children sticky with peppermint rock.

Sometimes they only went as far as the next sea-side resort. But the boldest of them might manage a Channel crossing, to let everybody have a glimpse of Boulogne. They were usually paddle steamers, making a great deal more fuss with all their churning than they made speed; and they weren't proud, for they let you see their works going round. They liked to call themselves 'Queens' and 'Belles': and even if they were new, there was always something old-fashioned, a Dickens touch, a mid-Victorian air, about them. They seemed to belong to the same ridiculous holiday world as pierrots and piers, sand castles, ham-and-egg teas; palmists, automatic machines, and crowded sweating promenades. But they were called out of that world – and, let it be noted – they were called out in good time and good order.

Yes, these 'Brighton Belles' and 'Brighton Queens' left that innocent foolish world of theirs – to sail into the inferno, to defy bombs, shells, magnetic mines, torpedoes, machine-gun fire – to rescue our soldiers. Some of them – alas – will never return. Among those paddle steamers that will never return was one that I knew well, – for it was the pride of our ferry service to the Isle of Wight – none other than the good ship 'Gracie Fields'. I tell you, we were proud of the 'Gracie Fields', for she was the glittering queen of our local line, and instead of taking an hour over her voyage, used to do it, churning like mad, in forty-five minutes. And now never again will we board her at Cowes and go down into her dining saloon for a breakfast of bacon and eggs. She has paddled and churned away – for ever. But now – look – this little steamer, like all her brave and battered sisters, is immortal. She'll go sailing down the years in the epic of Dunkirk. And our great grandchildren, when they learn how we began this War by snatching glory out of defeat, and then swept on to victory, may also learn how the little holiday steamers made an excursion to hell and came back glorious.

– from *Postscripts* –

I don't think there has ever been a lovelier English spring than this last one, now melting into full summer. Sometimes, in between listening to the latest news of battle and destruction, or trying to write about them myself, I've gone out and stared at the red japonica or the cherry and almond blossom, so clear and exquisite against the moss-stained old wall – and have hardly been able to believe my eyes; I've just gaped and gaped like a bumpkin at a fair through all these weeks of spring. Never have I seen (at least, not since I grew up) such a golden white of buttercups and daisies in the meadows. I'll swear the very birds have sung this year as they never did before. Just outside my study, there are a couple of blackbirds who think they're still in the Garden of Eden. There's almost a kind of mockery in their fluting.

I think most of us have often felt we simply couldn't believe our eyes and ears: either the War wasn't real, or this spring wasn't real. One of them must be a dream. I've looked out of my house in the country on these marvellous days of sun and blue air, and I could see the blaze and bloom of the Californian poppies and the roses in the garden; then the twinkling beeches and the stately nodding elms, and then, beyond, the lush fields and the round green hills dissolving into the hazy blue of the sky. And I've stared at all this – and I've remembered the terrible news of battle and destruction I'd just heard or read – and I've felt that one or the other couldn't be true.

Sometimes I've felt that I was really staring at a beautifully painted silk curtain; and that at any moment it might be torn apart – its flowers, trees and green hills vanishing like smoke, to reveal the old Flanders Front, trenches and bomb craters, ruined towns, a scarred countryside, a sky belching death, and the faces of murdered children. I had to remind myself that the peaceful and lovely scene before me was the real truth; that it was there long before the Germans went mad, and will be there when that madness is only remembered as an old nightmare.

Tennyson might have been prophesying this German madness in the spring when he wrote:

The fields are fair beside them,
The chestnut towers in his bloom;
But they – they feel the desire of the deep
Fallen, follow their doom.

But sometimes, too, I've felt that the unusual loveliness of our garden and meadows and hills has come home to us because these things are, so to speak, staring at us – as you see so many women now staring at their soldier husbands, sweethearts, sons, just before the trains take them away. It's as if this English landscape said: 'Look at me, as I am now in my beauty and fullness of joy, and do not forget.' And when I feel this, I feel too a sudden and very sharp anger; for I remember then how this island is threatened and menaced; how perhaps at this very moment, thin-lipped and cold-eyed Nazi staff officers are planning, with that mixture of method and lunacy which is all their own, how to project on to this countryside of ours those half-doped crazy lads they call parachute troops.

This land that is ours, that appeals to us now in all its beauty, is at this moment only just outside the reach of those self-tormenting schemers and their millions who are used as if they were not human beings but automata, robots, mere 'things'. They drop them from planes as if they were merely bombs with arms and legs. They send them swarming forward in battle as if they were not fellow-men but death-dealing dolls, manufactured in Goering's factories . . .

The Nazis understand – and it is their great secret – all of the contemptible qualities of men. They have a lightning eye for an opponent's weakness. But what they don't understand, because there's nothing in their nature or experience to tell them, is that men also have their hour of greatness, when weakness suddenly towers into strength; when ordinary easy-going tolerant men rise in their anger and strike down evil like the angels of the wrath of God.

– Eros and Logos –

1957

There are some people who become impatient and angry if they are confronted by large, loose, wild generalizations. (They can usually tolerate a few of their own: it is yours they object to.) Such people should not read what follows. It is not for them. I must point out, however, that the object of these pieces of mine is to provoke thought and discussion, chiefly by their refusal to treat routine topics in a routine fashion. They do not pretend to be the Word of the Lord, tablets of stone hauled down from the sacred mountain. I am merely trying to arouse the interest of the English-speaking middle class, overworked, worried, and on the edge of the last ditch. So I am capable of using anthropological and other terms that will set me at cross-purposes with some readers. For example: *matriarchy*. What do I mean when I suggest (partly out of devilment) that a matriarchy might save us?

Certainly I do not mean that Cabinet offices, the Judiciary, the Higher Command, the F.B.I., and the T.U.C. should be taken over as soon as possible by bustling, ambitious women. Nor that the images of fat fertility goddesses should be erected jointly by the Ministries of Works and Agriculture. What I am suggesting is that we should begin substituting, in our scheme of life, the values of the feminine principle, Eros, Yin, for those of the masculine principle, Logos, Yang. These are not identical with male and female. I am myself a fairly robust male but I am devoted to Eros rather than to Logos. Much modern literature, as widely different as the novels of Mr E. M. Forster and D. H. Lawrence, is a defence of Eros against Logos. On the other hand, many women, including the most aggressive feminists, are devotees of Logos, Yang girls. Not long ago I received a report of a women's conference in which the conclusions, which gave the impression that a woman was simply a neater, kinder sort of man, had clearly been arrived at under the spell of Logos. Those good ladies had not invited Yin to their conference: they probably knew she would not have behaved herself.

Risking the largest and wildest generalizations, let us consider the four Great Powers, America, Russia, Britain, and France, in terms of Eros and Logos, Yin and Yang. It is among the ironies of our time that the two main contestants, America and Russia, both represent societies that have too much Logos and not enough Eros. The rest of us have to choose not between Yin and Yang but between two Yangs. Which is yet another reason why we feel so uneasy, war or no war. We suspect that, whatever happens, Eros is out, not Yang.

Thus I cannot agree with my correspondent who

declared that America is a matriarchy. Appearances there are deceptive. Girls may be made much of, there may be much sentiment about Mother, woman (being widowed early) may own much of the wealth of the country, yet American society does not show us Eros triumphant. Its chief values are masculine values. The restlessness, ruthless ambition, emphasis on change, inventions, gadgets, mechanical progress, rather pedantic idealism, the idolatry of business, are all masculine, Yang stuff. That famous phrase 'The business of America is *business*' would seem to Eros the manifesto of a lunatic. Even the jazzing up of sex – the girls as 'quite a dish' – is Yang at work. (In the world of Eros it is the mature woman and not the young girl who is important.) Fifth Avenue shows us Logos bribing Eros with silks and gems. Woman in urban America has everything except the deep and lasting rewards of Eros. I once saw a party of middle-aged American women, lined, nervous, haunted, being shown a group of Indian squaws, smiling, fat, sleek as seals. The white women, encouraged by the woman guide, were pitying the red women, who had to do so much of the hard work. But the red women were not pitying themselves: they lived under Eros, and kept on smiling, with just a hint of feminine insolence. Of course, they would have liked to have had washing machines and four sets of nylon underclothes. But not at the Logos price, thank you. Hard work or no hard work, they were living in the right world.

Eros has to come in somewhere, of course, but if the masculine principle is supremely triumphant, not properly balanced, then Eros arrives in an inferior form. The result is a taste for crude sex and hard liquor, sex without personal relationship, drink as a short cut to unconsciousness. Naturally there are a great many Americans who dislike this style of life, but nobody who knows urban America and the literature (often very powerful) that represents it could deny that it is a style of life much in favour there. Eros throws the party when the serious work of the day has been done. When the Yang is tired, he phones for the Yin. But the masculine values are the real values, shaping and colouring society.

The essential Russian character, as displayed by its great literature and even by Party members after ten glasses of vodka in a room without microphones, belongs more to Eros than to Logos, though it has always been haunted by a kind of wild Logos spectre. (Those country houses in Turgenev show us both the Eros values and the Logos speculation.) But Russian Communism is Logos gone mad. Revolutions nearly always start in an Eros atmosphere, with much talk of private happiness, much love-making and the swearing of eternal friendships, and then soon swing over to Logos, with more laws, more police, more demands for instant obedience. A state that ignores the claims, which ought to be primary, of lovers, husbands and wives, parents and children, represents the Logos at work without any check from Eros. It destroys private happiness, all those relationships and styles of life that are at the heart of Eros, for the sake of a theory, or mere power, or some vague dream of happiness that has never been realized yet. To Eros this is the substance being destroyed for the shadow, and therefore sheer lunacy. If Russia is not a complete hell on earth, that is because Eros, the Yin values, still keep breaking through, though their activities are never on the agenda.

Here, to keep the balance, I must add my belief that a society entirely dominated by Eros would sink into stagnation and sloth, and oddly enough, I suspect, would begin to develop its own cruelties, Yin being as cruel in her way as Yang can be in his. But we need not worry about this state of things. Our immediate dangers are far on the other side. The Yang has his foot pressed down on the accelerator.

We are between two vast and powerful societies that are governed, each in its own way, by the masculine principle not reasonably balanced by the feminine. That such societies should be piling up atom bombs should surprise nobody. This is Logos on the spree. And it is significant that in both these societies the emphasis is on quantities of things rather than on the quality of personal experience. Soviet propaganda and American advertisements often seem to speak with almost the same voice: the management is different but the enterprise is broadly the same. If I must choose, I would prefer an American victory to a Russian one, just as I would prefer writing TV advertisements for Corn-flakes to lumbering on thin cabbage soup in Siberia. But I do not want either of these Yang-heavy societies which are less harmonious, less civilized, less capable of providing the deeper satisfactions, than the smaller and older communities they are dominating and then swallowing. We should have formed a neutral block, wearing the colours of the Yin, under the banner of Eros, who has not yet been completely banished from Western Europe.

Some people see in the Welfare State the handi-work of Eros. I wish I could agree with them. But though Welfare may belong to Eros, the State does not; and it seems to me that in the Welfare State the emphasis is on the State, with Logos firmly in com-mand. (And I cannot help wondering if some of the results of the Welfare State do not show the re-entry of Eros in an inferior form, creating a dim passivity.) There is, however, in British life still a suggestion that Yin is with us. We find traces of her in the flexibil-ity of our official machinery, in our lingering respect for private life, in a traditional piety towards earth, in the wealth of our odd hobbies and pastimes, in the wide network (to which we should cling) of our volun-tary associations. Eros still broods over much of our country life.

If we want to see more of Eros, we should look across the Channel. Much of the condemnation of the

French comes from the irritation felt by Logos for Eros. Try as they might to meet the Yang commitments, the French cannot help being guided by Yin values. That is why even the people who are most irritated by France, when they are discussing politics, want to spend their holidays there. They need the refreshment, the healing touch, of Eros. They want at least a little time away from the arid lunacies of Logos. And if I were a Frenchman, instead of being apologetic I would rise up in wrathful defence of my country's failure to turn itself into an efficient machine. I would declare that in our apparent Yin chaos, our wild Eros individualism, we were cherishing values that the other Great Powers were beginning to forget; that we were trying to preserve the sensible human scale; that we refused to sacrifice private happiness, discovered in the family, among lovers and friends, in the arts and genuine craftsmanship, for the public bosh, power, and statistics; that we still knew, if other people had forgotten, what deep satisfaction came from the service of Eros and the Yin. There are of course many things wrong with France, just as there are with the other three countries, but you can still find there a zest and a sparkle hard to discover in New York, Moscow, or London. It is the twinkle in the eye of Eros.

– On Education –

1957

When I was sixteen I left school and found my-self a job in a wool office. I had no intention of settling down in the wool business; I had already made up my mind to be a writer, and indeed was already writing hard; but clearly there was no living to be made out of writing for some years to come, so into the office I went. That I was allowed to remain there until I joined the army in 1914 is a tribute to my personality, which then, if not now, was a peculiar mixture of the insufferable and the enchanting; for there cannot have been many young clerks worse than I was in the long history of the wool trade. After about four and a half years in the army I received an ex-officer's grant that took me to Cambridge but by no means kept me there, even on a diet of bread and cheese and boiled eggs, so that I had to eke out with journalism, coaching, odd lectures, anything to earn a guinea or two. Finally, I left Cambridge for London, with some vague introduc-tions and capital of about forty-seven pounds.

Looking back, I can see quite clearly now that the great formative period for me was neither school nor the Cambridge years. It was 1911–1914, when no-body was trying to educate me nor paying for me to be instructed, when, in fact, I was working (though as little as possible) in the wool office. Our hours then were longer than most office hours are now: we had to be there at nine, took an hour for lunch, and usually finished sometime between six and seven. (If we worked after seven we received sixpence for tea money. No refreshment was provided before then.) We still sat on high stools like Dickens characters, and I was adroit at looking as if I were entering up the bag book, on my high desk, when in fact I was reading the poems of Yeats or Chesterton's last essays, lying inside my open drawer, which could be closed in a flash. I could also make a slower journey to and from the Bradford Conditioning House, losing myself in daydreams, than anybody else in the trade. Nevertheless, in spite of all these dodges, the office claimed me all the week and never let me go on Saturday until about half-past one. Nor did I live just round the corner from it, for our house, on the edge of the town, was at least two miles away. The fact remains, however, that this was the time when I learnt most and came along fastest. The State was not investing a penny in me.

(And here, for the benefit of those readers who believe in the State but not much in me, let me strike a rough balance. What have I had from the State? A very modest contribution towards my childhood and early youth, a grant that barely kept me alive at Cambridge, and a few fees for jobs undertaken from a sense of duty. What has it had from me? Fortunes in direct and indirect taxation, in Entertainment Tax on my plays and films, in foreign currency it badly needed, to say nothing about my services as a fighting soldier (no great shakes) in one war and as a day-and-night propagandist in another war. And if I should now go broke and dotty, I might receive with luck a Civil List pension of about two hundred a year. That is, if the country can afford it after meeting so many claims upon its generosity. I would have been ten times better off under George the Fourth.)

The truth is, I was fortunate during those years in my environment. My native city of Bradford is frequently mentioned, mostly by people who know nothing about it, as a kind of symbol of 'muck and brass', a stronghold of North-country narrow provincialism. But when I lived there, as a youth, it was considered the most progressive city in the kingdom. It was a Labour outpost. The first elementary school in the country where meals were provided was the one of which my father was headmaster. We had a Labour weekly to which, during this period, I contributed a regular page. Moreover, a number of Liberal German-Jewish families had settled there, as in Manchester, to give our West Riding dough a leaven of culture. Our Subscription Concerts followed the same plan as those at Leipzig. We also had our Permanent Orchestra and two great Choral Societies. We had three local daily papers as well as several weeklies. We had two theatres and two music-halls. We had a flourishing Arts Club and a Playgoers' Society. Our Central Lending and Reference Libraries were excellent. Bradford men were making their names in the arts and sciences. And though the town was ugly enough, the inviolable moors, where we walked and talked most weekends, began only a tuppenny tram-ride away. For a few pence more, taking a train, you reached the Dales, the most beautiful country-side in England.

So there we were, walking towards our vast sevenpenny teas, arguing over our pipes of fourpenny Navy Cut, listening to Nikisch and Busoni, Casals and Kreisler, for ninepence, seeing Little Tich and Grock for fourpence, reading H. M. Tomlinson in the local paper and Chesterton's Saturday essay in the *Daily News*, buying our shilling classics or Nelson's old sevenpenny series. I am not growling and grumbling again. For all I know to the contrary, lots of youngsters in their late teens are having as good a life now. Here I am not contrasting two periods. I am explaining why, in my considered judgement, these years, when I was neither in school nor college, turned out the most rewarding years I ever knew. It was, I repeat, because I was fortunate in my environment. It was not that I went to the right sort of school, but that I was living in the right sort of town. (Of course it might not have been right for you, but it was right for me.) In theory no doubt it was all wrong that a 'gifted youth' should spend his best years working long hours in a wool office. In practice it worked well. But it worked well, not because I happened to have massive determination and an iron will (I have never had either at any time), but because there was something in the atmosphere of that place at that period which encouraged me to develop and to grow. I do not think any school or college, by itself, could have done it. I would always have been wondering what was happening outside the walls. I would have been telling myself that this scholastic seclusion was not real life. I would not have taken anybody's word about what was going on in the outer world. But living as I did, I knew I was experiencing real life, exploring the outer world, taking what I wanted from my own town. Thus I was educating myself.

Let us take a look at what seem at first sight to be more formal processes of education. For example, at Oxford and Cambridge. In what lies their unique value? I would reply without hesitation that it lies in their successful creation (not quite what it used to be, perhaps) of an atmosphere of disinterested scholarship, an environment in which thought itself is triumphant. A young man can live for at least nine terms in a place that does not care a damn about the price of cotton and tin and the export trade. He can sit up all night arguing about God and Art. He can lock himself in, as I did once, with a tin of tobacco, a case of beer, and the whole of the Elizabethan Drama. In such places knowledge is in the very air. Not the formal courses of instruction but the atmosphere and the surroundings enrich the student. I have long thought it a shame that our students of music and acting have to live in London, lost among millions who care little or nothing for these arts. They would do much better if, as sometimes happens abroad, they received instruction in some place where the very landladies and bus drivers had a passion for music or the theatre, where the street outside was the ally of the school.

Now we have to spend so much on the school that we cannot afford to civilize the street. We are hoping that sooner or later the school will be strong enough to overcome the street, that a generation of teenagers will finally leave school to tear down the street and rebuild the town. If you argue with enthusiastic educationalists, they will admit under pressure that so far the street seems to have won, but they will declare their faith in the imminent victory of the school. I wish I could share this faith. But the odds seem to me too heavily in favour of the street, the town, the local environment. If their influence is not good, then the good influence of the school will not last long. To nine youngsters out of ten, the values of their home, their street, their town, seem far more important than anything learnt at school. There, outside, is real life, the world of the adults, towards which they are headed, away from the kid stuff of the classrooms. So it is largely a waste of time and money trying to persuade children that Shakespeare is our pride and joy if the town they live in cannot even boast one theatre, and prefers the films of Abbott and Costello to all that Shakespeare ever wrote. And if more and more youngsters leaving school want to read the *Daily Scream*, which steadily gets worse and worse, then what return is our national investment in education bringing? No doubt we need more teachers and should offer them better prospects. But what guarantee have we that they can successfully challenge the proprietors of the *Daily Scream,* the TV, radio and film experts, the advertising gang, the haters of the arts, the slow murderers of eager, hopeful living? Who, so far, is winning all along the line?

But no, I must not growl and grumble. I will simply state the case, as I see it. I owe most to a time when I was not being formally educated but when I enjoyed an environment favourable to a youth of my sort. I realize that youth still has its opportunities, perhaps more of them in some direction than I had, but it does seem to me that by and large the environment is far less favourable than it was, chiefly owing to the recent development of mass communications and of what might be called a mass pseudoculture. (Where comparison can be made, for example, with the popular Press, the decline is obvious.) Meanwhile, we spend more and more and more on Education, hoping rather desperately that somehow and sometime the values of the school will triumph over those of the streets outside the school. And this costs us so much that we cannot afford to change and improve the towns that receive our boys and girls after they have left school. The environment they know in their later teens, probably their most formative years, is a dreary mess of cheap commercial values, in which any fire kindled in the classroom is likely to be soon damped down and smothered. Perhaps the educationalists are right, and we have only to turn a corner. Perhaps I am an odd fish and cannot argue from my own experience. But I cannot help feeling thankful that I grew up before we had achieved such progress.

– Another Revolution –

1957

The other day, reading the Prologue to Collingwood's *Speculum Mentis,* I came to the following passage:

The actual output of pictures and statues, poems and string
quartets does not fail of its market because of its own low
quality; for the purchasers do not buy the best, because they
have not the skill to distinguish it; and anyone who doubts this
can prove it to himself by merely walking round an exhibition
of pictures and observing which of them are marked with red
seals . . .

This was written just over thirty years ago. Now
I have walked round a good many exhibitions of pictures during the last ten years, often prepared to buy
something I particularly liked, and it has been my experience that after the first few days, in an exhibition
that is selling at all, it is undoubtedly the best pictures
that bear the red seals and have already been bought.
The purchasers have changed since Collingwood's
time. They have probably less money but they have
better taste and judgement. There has in fact been a
revolution that, so far as I know, no social philosopher

anticipated, and that even now deserves more attention than it has received. And it might save some of us a good deal of time and temper if we understood what has happened and is still happening.

I do not know what is happening to other nations, but I am certain that among us English the visual appreciation of things has increased while the literary sense is decaying. Years ago I noticed that my own children lived more through the eye than I had done at their age, and that at the same time they did not lose themselves in books as I had done. It did not occur to me then that perhaps a general shift of attention was taking place. Now I am sure that what had happened in my family had also happened in thousands of others. These post-war years have shown us the results of this change. Whatever appeals first to the eye attracts immediate attention. The important art exhibitions, as we have seen, draw big crowds at once. Even the more modest shows, if they are fairly representative, are always well filled. More and more art books are published and sold, in spite of their high cost. There are more and more books in which the text is a mere excuse for the photographs. It is the popular illustrated periodicals that survive. People must have something to stare at, as the advertisers know. It is the demands of the eye that must be satisfied first. What was once chiefly the method of the kindergarten, to catch the attention of very young children, is now imitated far and wide, for every possible purpose.

Post-war entertainment proves the point over and over again. Ballet uses music, but its chief appeal is to the eye, and the popularity of ballet shows no sign of waning. (Even here in the Isle of Wight, where we do not even pretend to be in the movement, the only Arts Council import that paid for itself, I understand, was rather sketchy ballet.) The ice shows, which play to fantastic business, pipe out some indifferent words and music, but they are of course designed for the eye. In order to survive at all, the Theatre, especially in its larger productions, has had to seduce the visual sense, whatever might happen to the mind behind it. The most successful directors are visual directors, often working as if they were producing ballet and not drama. It is this fashion that is working havoc with some Shakespeare productions, which will omit some of his most exquisite poetry so that there is more time for pageantry and eye-filling antics. The Bard has almost been turned into a clothes-line. His newest directors, who seem to have no feeling for words, are ready to cut any other line.

The Film may have lost some ground as all-round entertainment during these last few years, but as a modest art form, as a visual creation of director and cameraman, it attracts more and more of the young. This is proved by the success of the British Film Institute and the hundred-and-one local societies it encourages. From the ballet the young London highbrows go swarming to any West End cinema showing a film that has been praised by the more austere critics, those concerned with visual values. Very few of these youngsters are to be found at any unspectacular play, no matter how original and powerful it might be. They no longer want words and ideas, not even those of Messrs Eliot and Fry. The visual sense must be fed and satisfied; they must have objective images, beautiful and significant if possible, but at a pinch almost any will do.

Finally – as the film boys say, the Big Pay-off – Television. Notice that it exists continually in a champagne atmosphere of ballyhoo and excitement that sound radio, even in its greatest days, never knew. Make two successful appearances in *Who's Your Father?* and the red carpets are rolled out from Lime Grove to the Caprice Restaurant. Here is the Giant Eye in fine frenzy rolling. One turn of a switch, and the images pour in. True, there may be words and music – and I will delightedly grant you that now this is anything but a 'land without music' – but ask any television producer what his first concern is. It is the visual sense that must be tickled and flattered first. And with this medium, delivered on any hearth-rug, we are as yet only making a rough-and-ready start: a choice of programmes, larger screens, colour and closer definition, all are yet to come and all have been promised. And because its own chief appeal is to the eye, then its programmes will tend to emphasize more and more what appeals to the eye in the world outside. The children are its slaves. So a huge generation not of readers or listeners but of viewers is now moving towards what we hope can be called maturity. Unless there should be a sharp reaction – always a possibility among us pendulum creatures – the final triumph of the visual sense is assured. In the end will be The Eye.

If you are looking at pictures, photographs, ballet, ice shows and other spectacles, films and television programmes, you cannot be curled up in a chair with a book. Moreover, the mind finds it hard to use its interior eye with a lot of noise about, and quiet corners are harder to find than they used to be. (Sooner or later, some of us will have to buy an instrument that can switch on silence instead of sound.) Indeed, many youngsters are now so accustomed to noise that a quiet room seems sinister and they have to bring a radio set or a gramophone into it, for sheer security's sake. In this atmosphere it is impossible for the art of literature to flourish. All the conditions and habits of mind are against it. The inner eye cannot be exercised. A feeling for words, a sense of their magical potency, can no longer be acquired. Some interest in ideas, on which the appreciation of literature also depends, is hardly felt at all. (It has been noted by educators, particularly in America, that too much visual instruction can make a youngster's mind unfit to grapple with abstract ideas.) So the necessary equipment of a genuine reader has not been assembled. The password that opens the old treasure cave has been forgotten.

Here some critics, in my view, do more harm than

good. These are the critics who take a lofty and some-
what arrogant stand, and seem to regard themselves as
the ferocious theologians and grand inquisitors of the
art. They announce, with that air of cold finality which
impresses undergraduates and repels their fathers and
mothers, that only a few books by a few carefully chosen authors can be regarded as Literature, and that all
else is rubbish on which no time should be wasted.
(The critic's own works, presumably, are an exception.)
Thus, Stendhal is Literature, Dumas is not; Henry
James is Literature, W. W. Jacobs is not. And nothing is gained, but much lost, by this hoity-toity treatment. It is better to assume that all writing not merely
informative, all poems, novels, essays, even criticism,
are *literature of a sort,* ranging from the shockingly
bad to the good and glorious. A lad who has enjoyed
Dumas may come to enjoy Stendhal. Jacobs, a genuine
artist in his own kind, may lead to James. Because, in
my youth, a lot of girls received at Christmas and birthdays their limp-leather editions of FitzGerald's *Omar*,
many of them went on to buy and read newer poets,
with the result that poetry found its way into the lists
of all good publishers. So long as there are readers,
trying this and that, there is hope for literature. It has
been our misfortune that just when reading itself, as a
pleasurable activity, was challenged, when the easier
visual sense began to be immensely catered for, we
should have developed a school of critics who spent
more time warning people away from literature than

encouraging them to enjoy it. They were the allies of the outer, not the inner, eye. If they are now appalled by the success of these visual things, partly at the expense of literature, it serves them right: they helped to steer people away from the bookshops.

Books come out, of course, and by the thousand, and publishers strangely multiply, to swell the chorus of *Ruin!* But it cannot be denied that we no longer behave as if we were primarily a literary nation. The space given to books and authors has dwindled. The mere attention, let alone the old excitement, is not what it was. (Dylan Thomas's tragic early death, more than his life and works, gave him sudden prominence.) To a writer the atmosphere of Paris seems quite strange now, because Paris is still a literary capital and London is not. Sartre, no towering genius, is capable of generating more excitement on both banks of the Seine than all of us could raise here, even if the whole Council of the Society of Authors marched along the Embankment in our underpants, making a last desperate appeal to the visual if not the literary sense. The grim harrying of the educated middle class, which has long been both the chief producer and consumer of literature, has done something for this revolution too. If our rulers were to be photographed holding a book instead of patting a racehorse, both the important political sections of our people, the magnates and the trade unionists, would feel that some contact with the great heart of the nation had been lost. But even what is left of that middle class, which has given us most of these bearded young men and untidy girls with horse-tail hair, has been seduced by the visual appeal, is growing up to expect its images to be created for it, is forgetting the ancient magic of words and any passion for ideas. Sometimes I think they are being encouraged to go this way – for it is not our old art that receives the sub-sidies – because they will be all the easier to handle. The busy eye is less rebellious than the lively mind. No barricades will be manned by montage enthusiasts, balletomanes, and the patrons of *Desert Song on Ice.* (And if publishers think they can still discover a few lively minds, what about putting a few of them in the dock, to be bullied by lawyers, then fined or impris-oned? That ought to rattle these fellows.) Meanwhile, we writers must accept the fact of this revolution. Soon we may have to take in one another's washing. It will be a change from trying to cut one another's throats.

– Televiewing –

1957

Down here on the island, where I have rented a fine large set and where we have a powerful transmitting mast not far away, I am a Viewer. We keep the set in a room originally intended for music, and I can sit in the dark there, viewing and viewing, without disturbing the rest of the household. I lie back in an armchair, put my feet up on a stool, and smoke and view away. Except when there are Test Matches, I do all my viewing after dinner. Wheezing a bit, heavy with food and drink, I waddle along the hall, switch on the set, drop into my chair and put my feet up, then peer into my magic mirror like a fourteen-stone cigar-smoking Lady of Shalott. At first I told myself that I watched the set and its antics for strictly professional and technical reasons, but lately I have not had even a shadow of that excuse. I am simply one of the Viewers. I have already passed uncounted hours half-hypnotized by the jiggling and noisy images. Sometimes I wonder if I am going out of my mind. We have been told that the worst is over after about four years, but long before that my outlook will have been so completely changed that I shall be a different person. I shall probably be removed to an old man's home.

Let us hope these places are equipped with good TV sets.

In my capacity as a Viewer, I have no intention of criticizing adversely and in detail the way things are done. Given this strange medium and their own particular responsibilities, the people directing and handling the medium do almost all that can be reasonably expected of them. Most of them, I know, are enthusiasts; if removed from TV they would feel they were in exile. I don't imagine I could do it better myself. I think I would be far worse than they are. Most of the familiar jeers and sneers at their efforts seem to me quite unfair. The difficulties they have to face are too lightly disregarded. The critics who attack them make little or no allowance for the black magic of the medium itself, always discussing the entertainment provided as if they had not been staring at a set but sitting in a theatre, a cinema, a concert hall, a cabaret. So not a word that follows must be taken as unfriendly criticism of TV personnel. Good luck to you, boys and girls! Thanks a lot, Mary, Peter, Sylvia, Derek!* But I am a Viewer too, one of the regular customers, even though I never ring up to complain that one of my precious prejudices has been ignored, and now I feel I must explain, as honestly as I know how, what the thing is doing to me.

* Mary Malcolm, Peter Dimmock, Sylvia Peters and Derek Hart, the first household names among BBC television announcers in the mid 1950s.

The general line about TV – I took it myself before I became a Viewer – is that it is terrifically exciting, immensely powerful, potentially very dangerous. Here is this miraculous medium that pours into the home, hour after hour, night after night, images so dazzling and enticing that it immediately outbids all other media for its tenancy of the mind and imagination. It can transform any licence-holder into a well-informed and thoughtful student of all public affairs. It can turn children into future scholars of Trinity and Girton or into gunmen and molls. So we are playing with fire and dynamite – but what fire, what dynamite! This is the kind of stuff I wrote and talked myself before I became a real Viewer. Now that I know what happens, I can no longer write and talk in this strain. Certainly the medium produces its own particular effects, un-doubtedly has an influence all its own; but these effects and this influence are very different from what they are generally imagined to be. Unless I am a very peculiar Viewer, the alarmists have all been looking in the wrong direction. They are like a man who expects a wolf at the door when he ought to be attending to the death watch beetle in the woodwork.

Install a set, turn a switch – and hey presto! – here in a corner of the living-room is an ever-changing image of the whole wide, glittering, roaring world. Or so they say. But that is not quite how my viewing works. To begin with, it does not seem to bring the outside world closer to me but pushes it further away. There

are times, after I have played the Lady of Shalott
longer than usual, when this world is not here at all;
I feel I am taking a series of peeps, perhaps from the
darkened smoke-room of a giant spaceship, at another
planet, with whose noisy affairs I am not involved at
all. Let me stare and idly listen long enough and I seem
to have arrived at some theosophical astral-body-life-
after-death. I am as little involved in or perturbed by
all these conferences, departures and arrivals of shadowy Ministers, crashes and floods, strikes and lock-
outs, aircraft and racing cars, atomic plants or fishing
villages, scientists and film stars, as some Great White
Master, a thousand years old, gazing into a crystal ball
in Tibet. At most, these are – as one of Yeats's characters observed in another connexion – the dreams
the drowsy gods breathe on the burnished mirror of
the world. I remember an old retired nannie, rather
weak in the head, who when she visited the silent films
thought everything she saw was part of one vast con-
fused programme, an astonishing but acceptable mixture of the Prince of Wales and cowboys and Indians
and Stanley Baldwin and sinking ships and *It*-girls and
the Lord Mayor of London. She was an early Viewer.
I know now exactly what she felt. Perhaps I am rather
weak in the head too.

No sooner is any subject under review and discussion on the screen than it is drained of all reality. The instrument itself, probably guided by some
satanic intelligence hostile to our species, adds a fatal

dream effect. Even what I thought were urgent burning problems stop being problems at all. They are not settled, but their hash is. Somehow I no longer care what happens about Oil or Married Women At Work or Youth And The Churches Today or What We Do With The Old People or Whither Britain. I just view them. They might be bits from untidy and badly acted plays. Sometimes I don't know – and don't care – if the gesticulating image of a Foreign Minister belongs to a real Foreign Minister or to an actor in one of those political plays we are always having. Here on the screen the difference between Yugoslavia and Ruritania is hardly worth bothering about. After half an hour of The Future Of Our Fisheries or Africa At The Crossroads, the programme personalities, bursting with fisheries or Africa, stare accusingly at me and ask me what I propose to do about, it. They might as well know now that, as a Viewer, I don't propose to do anything about it. After they have given me a final earnest look and asked their last question, I stare at the credit titles, listen dreamily to the end music, wonder idly why Malcolm Muggeridge looks handsomer on the screen than off, where Woodrow Wyatt has acquired his new haughty accent, light another pipe, and float into the next programme.

Perhaps it is *Picture Parade* or something of the sort, in which all the imbecilities of the film studio hand-outs and the fan magazines are given a kind of idiot dream life, especially – ah what golden moments!

– in the foyer at a gala première where celebrities of screen and stage consent to smile at us and tell us how exciting it all is, as if we didn't know, and are wished lots of luck. As a Viewer I try not to miss one of these occasions.

To view one, smoking in the darkened room with your feet up, is much better than actually being there, what with all the dressing up, the heat and fuss, the pushing and shoving to get nearer the mike or the Press photographers. It is a dream glimpse, carefully focused and timed, of a dream world. But it is all so *exciting*, as everybody keeps telling us Viewers. Perhaps that is why I so often find myself laughing – all alone, there in the dark – probably only a nervous excitement.

Some nights there seem to be dozens and dozens and dozens of people being interviewed, not just about films but about everything. We go all over the place – inside and outside Ministries, home and abroad, to airports and railway stations, to sports grounds and factories. The organization of it all, the sheer technical achievements, are a credit to our civilization. The courtesy and friendliness are admirable: all the persons interviewed are for ever being thanked and wished good luck. People under Cabinet rank and sixty years of age are on Christian name terms at once. It is a wonderful and happy world, this of TV interviews. And perhaps that is why it is not a world in which anybody ever says anything. That might spoil it. Between the cordial 'Hello's' and the charming 'Good-byes' nothing much seems to happen. We are either going to the interview or coming away from it. 'Let us,' they say proudly, 'go to Coketown and talk to the Mayor himself – so now *It's Over to Coketown* – This is Coketown and here in the studio is the Mayor of Coketown, who has kindly consented to talk to us – Very good of you, Mr Mayor – er what about this er campaign of yours, Mr Mayor? – Well, Reg, I think er I can say er we here in Coketown er hope to get it started fairly soon – Thank you, Mr Mayor, and the best of luck – Thank you, Reg – And now we return you to London – This is London and that was the Mayor of Coketown being interviewed by our representative, Reg Rowbottom – and *now* –'

At first, when I was a new Viewer, a stranger in this magic world, I wanted the Mayor to say something, if only to justify all the trouble that had been taken to flash his image across the country. Now I know that this does not matter at all, that what is important is that we should keep jumping around, stare at a fresh face for a moment or two, then be off again. The instrument likes to do this, and it is the instrument that has us in its power. In this world of the magic tube, all the values are different. Here we are more interested in what the interviewer sounds and looks like than we are in what the interviewed person says. Viewing, I accept these topsy-turvy values. It is only afterwards, coming to my senses and thinking things over, I begin to question them. Staring at the set, my mind almost a blank, I am quite ready to believe in TV personalities, the elite and aristocracy of thin dream world. I do not ask what they have done, what massive talents they possess. They still have personalities where I, as a Viewer, a captive of the screen, have little or none. Not this Christmas but possibly the next, when I may have said good-bye to reality, I shall have no party of my own, perhaps will no longer understand what arrangements could be made for one; I will attend, as a Viewer, a party of TV personalities, to enjoy the sparkle of the wine in their glasses, to listen with joy to the crunching of their mince pies; and one or two of them may look straight in my direction, to wish me a Merry Christmas Programme, a Happy New Year's Viewing.

Meanwhile, sitting in the dark with my feet up, I feel I have *had* Fisheries or Africa or Youth And The Churches Today. I couldn't agree more about Married Women At Work or What We Do With The Old People or Whither Britain, and could hardly care less. We Viewers know now that we are such stuff as dreams are made on, that all is Maya, that *For in and out, above, below, 'Tis nothing but a magic shadow-show*. So it is easy to imagine oneself viewing the next war, dreamily watching whole cities crumble to radioactive dust, catching a last glimpse of Manchester or Leeds in between a thirty-minute detective play and some light music and a gipsy dancer. Never did a medium of information and entertainment arrive more opportunely, to soothe the tormented mind, to ease the bewilderment of the soul. We may emerge from our four or five years' bondage to it, having at last achieved detachment, for ever untroubled and smiling, finally victorious over the technique and the instrument. Already we Viewers, when not viewing, have begun to whisper to one another that the more we elaborate our means of communication, the less we communicate. Some words on a page can be unforgettable. The memory of an actor, moving and speaking on a platform, may haunt us all our lives. Then the inventors and technicians arrive, the costs rise prodigiously, the complication sets in, and we get film and radio, far less potent and memorable. The inventors and technicians, in a frenzy, with millions of money behind them, invade the home with TV, adding more and more images to sound, performing miracles with time and space, bringing in colour, stereoscopic sight, everything. And out of this mountain of invention and technique, finance and organisation, comes a little dream mouse. 'Not bad,' we Viewers cry. 'What next?'

– Women Don't Run the Country –

from the *Saturday Evening Post*, 12 December 1964

A thousand times I must have read or heard that American society is now a matriarchy. I disagree. Here I may be told I am not an American, don't live here and only pay occasional visits. My personal opinions may not be important, but if I can persuade a few hundred thousand readers that this matriarchy idea is all wrong, I shall be doing this country a great service. The saving in analysts' fees might soon amount to several million dollars a year.

Nobody believes, of course, that America is a matriarchy in the anthropologists' sense of this term: 'A state or stage of social evolution in which descent is reckoned only in the female line, all children belonging to the mother's clan.' In such a society the chief deities would be Mother Goddesses, magically potent symbols of fertility. (In many places they began to be ousted by several law-making male deities about three thousand years ago.) What a large number of men do believe, however, is that America is well on its way to becoming a new kind of matriarchy, increasingly ruled by mothers and dominated by Woman. In a superficial sense, American women do seem to have the upper hand. They appear to call the tune while their men pay the piper. They sweep in triumph along Fifth Avenue. This is their place, their hour. But it is all mere surface fuss, a little almond icing on the cake. In its fundamental values, tone, organization, American society is moving *away* from rule by Woman. American women make a fuss because they find themselves in a *man-made* society. The men who denounce this fuss should criticize the society they have created, and stop talking nonsense about women.

In a matriarchy it is feminine and not masculine values that are dominant. In such a society women feel completely at home. It provides the kind of life they want. It is shaped and coloured by Woman's deepest feelings. It satisfies not her superficial wants – a washing machine, a new TV set – but her profoundest needs. What are these needs? They are not concerned with things at all; they are concerned with personal relationships. Woman enjoys things – furs, gowns – simply as toys of love, which to her is *the* gigantic blazing reality, compared with which defence, invention, politics, legal and financial systems are simply so much masculine hocus-pocus. In a true matriarchy, love, personal relationships, home-making, family-creating and taking root in a settled society are at the top of all lists of priorities. They come first, and all the things that men are always arguing about come a very bad second.

A matriarchy is always a small society, deeply rooted in the earth and in tradition and custom. It would never attempt large-scale industry because one of the first things that such an industry does is to break up families. Then it keeps people moving about and prevents them from sinking any roots. All this, from the matriarchal point of view, is not progress but a barbarous invasion of the kingdom of love. It puts things before people, and in the feminine scale of values, this is a terrible crime, the ultimate treason.

I suspect that in most matriarchies the women work hard and the men take it easy. This should not surprise anyone who remembers that in these societies sexual love is much more important than business. A wife who sees her husband primarily as a lover, not as a provider, does not want him to work until he is ready to drop. A tired man makes a poor lover. And a man for ever worried will not make the best husband and father.

In a matriarchal system a woman might toil for the comfort and well-being of her family, but she would see no sense in drudging away to add to the profits of some vast corporation. And we can bet our boots that in such a system nobody would be encouraged to travel at supersonic speeds, to land on the moon, to invent devices for destruction on the largest possible scale. These elaborate imbecilities are the products of the masculine mind, and they would not be tolerated in a society run by women. Men who even dreamed up such ideas, much less demanded that everybody make sacrifices on their behalf, would be given a very rough time by the females in charge.

Whatever else may be said about the character of contemporary American society, it certainly represents the triumph of the masculine principle. Nor is it hard to see why this should be so. American traditions, from Puritanism to pioneering, are severely masculine. The immense development of industry upholds the masculine principle. The emphasis upon invention and machinery and the prominence given to finance and commerce, characteristic of America, are essentially male. And up to now American society has been steadily offering Woman not more and more but less and less of what she really wants. Never were her superficial needs more elaborately attended to. Never were her deepest needs so often ignored. Remember, what she really wants is not a lot of 'things', but love, a secure family life, taking root in a stable community. And nine times out of ten she has a longing to be close to living, growing things, and does not want to find herself on some vast plain of cement.

Why do American men imagine that their society is turning into a matriarchy? It is because their women demand so much attention, spend so much on themselves, invade one masculine region after another, and now exercise tremendous economic power. (This last point is often because husbands overwork and worry themselves into early graves. In a matriarchy, these men would have been encouraged to take it easy, for most women prefer live husbands to blocks of shares and seats on the board.)

It is precisely because they find themselves in an alien society that so many American women demand so much attention. If this society represented their own deepest values, they would feel at home in it and therefore they would not be crying, 'Look at me. Attend to me.' They feel that unless they make a fuss, they will be in danger of disappearing from sight, like wives who have gone with their husbands to inspect some vast new machine which is entrancing to the male.

It is true that far more is spent on feminine adornment in America than anywhere else on earth. There are two reasons for this, and neither of them even suggests that women rule America. The first is that this immense trade in feminine frippery is good for business, oiling innumerable wheels of production and consumption. But this idea of an ever-increasing turnover, together with the colossal amount of sheer waste, is itself essentially masculine and, I suspect, repugnant to Woman on her deeper levels, where she is a frugal creature. In societies that approach the matriarchal, the women are not for ever buying new clothes but tend to be conservative about their dress, preserving through generations the same native costumes. Behind the whirl of fashion in America are men who are keeping an eye on their balance sheets.

The second reason for all this feminine adornment is that women are indulged just because they are in an alien society. They are like girls in a mining camp being rewarded with gold nuggets. Because they are out of place, they must be given a treat. Moreover, the woman elaborately adorned is a kind of tribute to the male, who can show her off. The natural woman enjoys dressing up occasionally, but she does not see herself as a kind of model. What she wants is an erotic relationship, offering her emotional security, a relationship in which she is clearly seen, appreciated, loved, *as a person*. And if she is accepted and loved as a person, she does not want to be expensively dressed up all the time – this is the illusion of men who do not see women as real people – and can be quite happy messing about in an old housecoat and wearing no makeup.

If American women often do make excessive demands – and here I am only repeating what I have heard many American men say – this may be a kind of revenge. They marry men who wear themselves out, make themselves unfit for conjugal companionship – but not for something noble and glorious, to which a woman can also dedicate herself, but for something that by the feminine principle seems contemptible and ridiculous – like selling 100,000 more boojums this year than last. It is worth pointing out here that nearly all courageous and truly dedicated men, not engaged in merely increasing profits, arouse intense feminine loyalty. It is the men who grind themselves away on ignoble and idiotic work who largely have to meet women's excessive demands. If Man has turned himself into a provider, then let him do more and more providing. If he believes cars and fur coats are more important than kisses and companionship, then she will demand bigger cars and richer fur coats. *But this is not what she really wants.*

It has been said – and here again I am only repeating what I have heard many times – that too many American women are sharply aggressive in an unfeminine way. And this aggressiveness has been put forward as proof of the growth of a matriarchy here. And again, this is completely wrong. It is precisely because American society reflects masculine and not feminine values that so many women become aggressive. They are putting on aggression as they would put on fur coats and boots in an Arctic climate. If their world seems to them so determinedly masculine, then they feel they must adopt male characteristics. It is no use speaking in soft, gentle tones if everybody else is shouting. To make themselves heard at all, then they must shout too. Deep down they do not want to be aggressive but the manner is forced on them. And this makes for further dissatisfaction, and this in turn may mean that the aggressive manner is now heightened. It is our old enemy – the vicious circle.

During the last fifty years American women, chiefly through inheritance, have come to possess a formidable amount of economic power. This is a country of rich widows. The extent of their influence has helped to create this legend that women are in charge. But this does not go down to the roots of American society, does not change its fundamental character: it is still dominated by the masculine and not the feminine principle. How do I know? Well, here is a quite simple test. At the present time America possesses sufficient instruments of destruction to kill every man, woman and child on earth. This macabre achievement, which has demanded an astonishing amount of technical skill and superb organization and the expenditure of billions and billions of dollars, not only represents the masculine principle triumphantly asserting itself but also suggests the male mind coming to the end of its tether. Where is the feminine principle, where is Woman, in this madness? Where is the feminine emphasis here upon love, on the happiness of persons? Is this how women want their money spent? We have only to ask the question to know the answer. Here is a society shaped and coloured by male values. It is about as much like a matriarchy as the Marine Corps.

Now here I must make an important point. If I say, as I do, that a swing over from the masculine to the feminine principle is now urgently necessary, I do not mean that women must leave the professions and the businesses and return to the kitchen and the nursery. (After all, I am married, and most happily married, too, to a brilliant archaeologist and writer, who has her own career.) What I do mean is that society itself must be as thoroughly permeated by womanliness as it is by masculinity, that *as a community,* not simply as separate persons, we must accept feminine values with their emphasis upon love, people, relatedness, synthesis as opposed to analysis, intuitiveness as distinct from purely intellectual discourse.

We live in a sick world. It is sick because it is now hopelessly unbalanced. It is unbalanced because the masculine principle has been given too much freedom and the feminine principle has been fettered and stifled. This means that women feel frustrated and unhappy. And women who feel frustrated and unhappy find it hard to bring to men that idea of relatedness, that sense of wholeness, which most men ask from Woman. For the *psychological need* of each sex for the other (which women understand better than men) is unfathomably deep, going down to the very roots of our being. America is not a matriarchy, and I do not think it ever will be. But it will be a good day for both men and women when America begins to behave as if it *wanted to be a matriarchy,* turning from the bleak insanity of the unchecked masculine principle to the glow and warmth of the feminine principle, from the icy glare of Logos to smiling Eros.

– The Moments –

1966

All my life, I now realize, I have been nourished and secretly sustained by certain moments that have always seemed to me to be magical. If I have completed the tasks and shouldered the burdens all the way, finishing the marches without handing over my rifle and pack or dropping out, it is neither conscience nor energy that has kept me going but the memory and the hope of this magic. It has visited me before; it will come again. Sooner or later I would taste the honey-dew once more. And if this is to have a romantic temperament, then I have a romantic temperament. If there is immaturity here, then I am still immature in my seventy-first year.

But here I shall fire a few rounds in the direction of the enemy camp. People who in their confident maturity reject this magic, who have instant 'nothing-but' explanations of everything, are either kept going by their vanity – and the vanity of severely rational persons is astounding – or not sustained at all, existing hungrily in despair, seeking power at all costs, trying various brutal excesses, or stiffening into automata. I can imagine an age, in which this magic has been explained away, that would cover the world with zombies all manipulated and directed by power-maniacs. In such an age, power and organization and machinery would be everything, poetry would be nothing. How far off is it?

Sometimes I have wondered if the seemingly inexplicable *rages* of the young, violently destructive now in so many different countries, might not be explained by the non-arrival of these magical moments. Something expected, promised at birth, is missing. Where among all these prompt deliveries of Grade-A pasteurized is the milk of Paradise? However, it is true that for one lad who is breaking windows there are a hundred, not mentioned in the papers, who never pick up a brick. And it is not for me to say that our Pop culture never brings its magical moments. But what is certain is that it does not attempt the grand and sublime, which is what we cry out for in our youth. On the other hand, it is equally certain that whenever the Eroica or the Choral Symphony is being performed, the cousins of the brick-throwing lads will be there, if necessary standing for hours. The contemporary scene is now so wide and complicated that anything can be proved from it. I must return to myself.

Describing an innings by Jessup, Neville Cardus wrote: 'He at once took the game out of the prison of cause and effect.' That is what these moments have always done for me. That is why they are magic. Two and two suddenly make twenty-five. In a flash they add another dimension to existence. They award us, for as long as they last, a bonus, huge, irrational, glorious. We win a prize from God knows where. It isn't earned and deserved; that would be justice or fair dealing, a decent cause producing a satisfactory effect; whereas this is magic. It belongs to the fairytale world, in which the idlest of the three lads in the forest meets the princess, and hardly anything that happens could be explained by experts writing in the weekly journals. Indeed, the moments are entirely beyond the reach of experts, who, I am convinced, never experience them. They favour the woolly minded, of whom, I am proud to declare, I am one. Brush away all wool, give yourself a first-rate razor-sharp intellect, and you will go far, and probably a hell of a long way from this magic. This is one reason why men who have arrived where they have always wanted to be are impressive but not much fun to be with, so that their women so often look depressed. Whatever they may say, women believe in a magical world. They are seen in the prison of cause and effect only on visiting days.

It is my experience that these moments arrive as and when they choose. They cannot be summoned, nor even induced, beckoned. But of course some circumstances are more favourable than others. It is just possible I might be visited by one of these moments while reading a report on the tin-plate industry or a list of arthritic patients in Bedfordshire, but all odds are heavily against it. On the other hand, I have found the arts most generous with these magical moments, and this is one good reason – there are several others, mark you – for hanging around with them. If this last phrase suggests an absence of painstaking study, anxious application, then it is doing what I intended it to do. I suspect – though of course I am writing within the limits of my own temperament – that you have to hold yourself a bit loosely, not bothering about cultural improvement, for the magic to work.

In the long run, which is where I am now, music has worked best for me, though when I was younger I think literature and drama were neck-and-neck with it. The visual arts have given me enormous enjoyment – and indeed I am a bit of a holiday painter myself – but for some reason obscure to me they have rarely brought me these magical moments. Perhaps my ear provides a shorter cut to enchantment than my eye. Certainly music may do the trick when it is far below its highest level. Let nobody imagine I have to wait for Bach's B minor Mass or Beethoven's late quartets. To give the first example that occurs to me – and I could offer dozens – in the opening movements of his Cello Concerto and his D minor Symphony, Dvorak makes his woodwind trail after his main themes – they are like sunlit wisps of dissolving cloud – and to this day the magic has not utterly faded from them. Again, listening recently to a new recording of Elgar's First Symphony (which I had long thought I didn't care for), I found that with the muted trombones at the end of the third movement, the Adagio, the sudden magic seemed almost numinous, as if the gods walked the earth again. Enough, enough!

How far and with what complexity and depth the arts interact with life, we do not know, though some brave writers – Proust, for instance – have refused to avoid the subject. It may be that people who know and care nothing about the arts have known as many magical moments as the rest of us have – perhaps even more if they happen to be introverts living in lonely places. (But probably far fewer if they happen to be ambitious politicians, editors of sensational newspapers, brisk salesmen, New York taxi drivers.) There seems to me no difference in quality between the moments coming by way of the arts and those that arrive, quite unexpectedly, in our ordinary daily life. These are more remarkable than the immensely heightened moments of travel, of which most of us could furnish examples – and perhaps too often do. In my life I have suddenly known the greatest happiness always when *there was no apparent reason for it* – when out of nowhere there came floating up the great blue bubble. I shall never forget walking once, some years ago, along Piccadilly and across Leicester Square in a blinding snowstorm, which made walking difficult and did not seem to me at all picturesque and romantic, and yet I walked the whole way in a kind of ecstasy, as if in another world, magical and immortal. And there was no reason for it at all, not the tiniest scrap of any possible cause.

It is the same, at least in my experience, with personal relationships. I have never needed any help from manuals on how to get rich in the private commerce between the sexes; but even so, I think we are now inclined to make too much out of the bedroom scenes in our love stories. It is my experience that even in love the magical moments come when they please, often when we are wearing all our clothes and are far from the bedroom. I can remember a moment of complete insight and perfect understanding, as if one had been given the freedom of a strange continent, that arrived in a dreary little teashop near the ministry from which I had extracted the lady of my choice. There were not even any words, just a meeting of eyes above the tea-cups, but a magical meeting, in which there was the promise of many happy years, an unearned bonus if there ever was one.

So long as we experience these moments, we live in a magical world. (And don't let anybody talk you out of it, boy.) I was arguing the other day with a clever young man who said that we are machines – extra-ordinarily elaborate, intricate, delicate, subtle – but machines. I said that we weren't so long as we remained open-ended, with one end open to the collective un-consciousness, the whole heritage of earth life, and the other open to influences beyond our understanding. And perhaps it is when we are suddenly opened a lit-tle more at either end that two and two seem to make twenty-five, another dimension is added, we taste the honey-dew, and all is magical. Of course the moments do not arrive as often as they did, but I soldier on in the belief that I have not yet used up my ration, that there are still a few more to come.

– Tobacco –

1966

I have just realized that I have been smoking a pipe
for half a century. I grew up among pipe smokers;
my father was one and so were most of his friends. Fifty
years ago in the north there were still some real tobacconists, who knew how much Latakia and Perique to
add to Virginia, who did not earn a living by hiring
girls to push packets of cigarettes across the counter.
In those days men offered their tobacco pouches to
one another. Some of them in the north may still do it,
but not for years and years have I given or received a
fill. Perhaps I don't live right.

To this day you will find pipe tobacco improves
as you move up the map. It is better in the north of
England than it is in the south. In Scotland it is better still. The Scots like to boast, but it is strange they
never mention the debt owed to them by the world's
pipe smokers. There is some good tobacco in Ireland
too. On the Continent, especially in the northern
half, there has been some improvement since the war;
but most of it, now got up to look British, is still very
poor stuff. Most American pipe tobacco is too sweet,
as if meant for eating not smoking. I remember that
George Doran, the publisher, used to smoke a Los

Angeles mixture that had a chocolate flavour. If any pipe-smoking reader is planning to stay in America, he should make a note of a mixture, medium and broad-cut, that comes from St Louis and is called Hayward Mixture. I have carried yellow pound tins of it into almost every state of the Union. Sometimes when I wondered if I was going out of my mind, a few pipes of it have restored my sanity.

When I started smoking a pipe, fifty years ago, I bought Cut Cavendish from Salmon and Gluckstein at 3½d. an ounce. It was very strong, and there were times when, after puffing furiously as youngsters near-ly always do, I felt queasy and my surroundings began to shift about and dissolve. Since that hard begin-ning, I have been able to smoke anything, though not of course always with enjoyment. But I would rather have bad tobacco than no tobacco. In Egypt, earlier this year, I was compelled to smoke some of their local muck, wondering as I coughed and cursed why the United Arab Republic, which you are never allowed to forget for a moment, did not make sure that Syrian to-bacco reached Egypt. Probably President Nasser does not smoke a pipe.

Those people now ready to write and tell me I am a slave to a dirty habit need not waste time, paper and stamps. I admit I have been long enslaved by tobac-co. But all men are enslaved by something, and there are worse masters than the weed. By encouraging me to reflect, at the same time freeing me from spiritual pride, it has kept me from more dangerous forms of slavery. Nor have I ever been able to see that smoking is a particularly dirty habit. It is absurd of course, this continuous puffing out of smoke, but no dirtier than most of our habits. You have only to be sufficiently fastidious, and life itself is one huge dirty habit. Purity is reached only in the crematorium.

We are told, usually by people who dislike tobacco, that smoking injures the health. That may be so, though it is worth pointing out that the contributions to a world civilization of men careless of their health far exceed those of the health-seekers. (*Fit for what?* still seems to me the best joke *Punch* ever achieved.) There may be something in this lung cancer idea. Yet when I was young, and good tobacco was far less than a tenth of the price it is now, I was surrounded by heavy smokers, but nobody seemed to be suffering from lung cancer.

I suspect a good deal of disguised puritanism among medical men, especially in America. They denounce various forms of enjoyment but never suggest that the whole modem way of life is idiotic. A man who sits with ten telephones in Wall Street, desperately trying to outwit his competitors, might be healthier if he did not smoke, did not drink, ate no fats. He would be healthier still if he got to hell out of Wall Street and forgot the rat race.

But look at the money we waste on tobacco. No, madam, in Britain we are not spending all that money on tobacco, but on taxes. If we all stopped smoking tomorrow, several hundred million would have to be found elsewhere, for rockets that must never be fired and other imbecilities. The ever-increasing duties on tobacco, making its price about twelve times what it was when I started smoking, show our Establishment at its worst – uncreative, lacking all ingenuity, lazy-minded, mean and callous. I am not thinking of myself now, when I call this completely inequitable taxation mean and callous. I am thinking of men of my generation trying to keep going among the never-had-it-so-goods on wretched tiny pensions.

You are seventy and have always enjoyed a smoke. Now, no longer active and with a lot of time on your hands, you enjoy a smoke more than ever. To ponder and remember over a pipe is probably now your greatest pleasure. So what do they do to you, these smirking Chancellors of the Exchequer, with their annual Budget performance, these first-class minds of the Treasury, the pick of Oxford and Cambridge? Every time they need more money, they empty your tobacco pouch, robbing you of the last enjoyment life offers you. There is no fire in the grate, the cupboard is nearly bare; the road at the end of the street is noisy and dangerous with cars; your friends are dead or dying; so they screw another sixpence out of you, before you are carted away to rot in an overcrowded understaffed hospital; and if you haven't the sixpence then you suck an empty pipe while you read, in the paper you borrowed, all about the tax-free millions that have been made out of property deals.

In restaurants all pipe smoking is sharply discouraged, not because of the food, cigar smoke being even stronger, but probably because there is no profit to be made out of it. (The profit on cigars is fierce.) It is the banning of the pipe from aeroplanes – and I bet the British started that – which has brought me hours of misery. Only on the old Stratocruisers could one go below to the little bar and light a pipe, and more than once I have bumped across the Atlantic, reading and smoking the night away while all the other passengers were asleep. On one flight, without the little bar below, I was able to smoke my pipe all the way to Montreal, but that was because I had deliberately chosen a Friday the thirteenth and had the plane almost to myself. This does not mean I am not superstitious. I was born on a thirteenth and so feel free of its sinister influences.

Pipes of course can smell foully, though the worst of them are probably more easily endured than the reek of the last inch or so of soggy cigars. To my mind the gravest offender is that favourite of all authorities – the cigarette. It is not the tobacco but the paper that is so offensive. A room crowded with cigarette smokers is like a papermill on fire. Again, it is not the cigarette that is being smoked that afflicts eyes, nose and throat, but the cigarette smouldering in the hand or on the ash tray, the Virginian joss stick. The behaviour of cigarette smokers has always puzzled me. Why, for example, do they want to light up ten seconds before a meal, then puff again between meat and pudding? Many of them, I feel, do not consciously enjoy smoking, as I most genuinely do, but wish to avoid the pain of not smoking. I do not include them among the friends of tobacco.

Cigars can be things of beauty, works of art, but on this level they are harder and harder to find, evil entropy being at work here as elsewhere. (This is called by my friends Iris and John Bayley 'Jack's Law'.) On a much lower level I would now just as soon smoke a Jamaican cigar as a Havana; and I have spent many a pleasant hour abroad – never finding them in London – with those large black Brazilian cigars, banded a threatening scarlet and emerald green, that are so surprisingly mild and friendly, as if some flashing-eyed Carmen in a gipsy cave came across, took your hand, and talked quietly and sensibly.

A cigar rounds off a substantial meal, but when, being short of pipe tobacco in distant places, I have found myself compelled to smoke them all day, I have soon got tired of them. Perhaps if Sir Winston, round about 1944, had taken to a pipe, we might have all been living today in a happier world. But the pipe smoker's appearance of solidity and wisdom is of course illusory. Some of the biggest chumps I have ever known have had pipes stuck in their faces. Even so, I fancy they were great relighters and puffers and knockers-out of dottle, and perhaps never filled a pipe when they were by themselves. There is a kind of pipe smoking that belongs to actors on the stage and clergymen having a jolly good yarn with the chaps.

It is just possible that a few readers may decide either to try smoking a pipe for the first time or, what is more likely, to have yet one more shot at it. To them, after this half century, I venture to offer some advice. Many men have defeated themselves as pipe smokers. They start the wrong way. They buy a small light pipe and probably fill it with some rubbed-out yellow flake, at which they puff away. In a few minutes they have a furnace in their hands and too much saliva in their mouths; there is no fragrance, no flavour; the pipe, almost too hot to hold, begins to gurgle disgustingly; so they decide pipe smoking is not for them – 'Tried but can't manage it, old boy – wet smoker.' I would be one as well with that equipment.

To begin with, do not buy one pipe but at least three. If you cannot afford pipes by well-known makers, do not buy cheap imitations but search the tobacconists' for throwouts. Some of the best pipes I have ever had I have picked out of the baskets of throwouts. Here I must add, after my fifty years, that just as you choose a pipe, so a pipe chooses you. I have had as presents magnificent pipes, cut from the finest straight-grain briar, that never gave me ten minutes' satisfactory smoking. Either they were not right for me or I was not right for them. There is something like a personal relation here. And until you are used to smoking a pipe, avoid small thin light pipes: they get hot too quickly.

You will be happier at first with fairly large pipes, even if they seem too heavy. And do not scrape out all the carbon, for it keeps the pipe cool.

But why three pipes? Because you must never refill a warm pipe: it is precisely this that has left us pipe smokers in bad odour. I have watched with horror men smoking the same pipe hour after hour, smelling like gardeners' bonfires. Always I carry three pipes in my pocket. On my desk there may be a dozen or more. I buy and use a great many pipe cleaners. On the other hand, I remove from all pipes any aluminium tubes or similar devices. I have been sent pipes that had most ingenious arrangements for collecting nicotine, but they always seemed to me to taste nasty. The pipe, I suspect, is an enemy of gadgetry.

Now for the tobacco. Do not make a start with light Virginia leaf or mild mixtures. They can easily be hot and tongue-burning, fry a darker flake or a mixture with a fair amount of Latakia and Perique in it. Out of the strong comes forth sweetness. Fill your pipes carefully, using the third finger not the first to complete the filling. The trick then is to keep the tobacco smouldering, smoking as slowly as possible, for the hotter it is the worse it tastes and smells.

A cool clean well-packed pipe that is just being kept alight pleases the smoker and anybody who comes near him. All over the world people have said to me, 'What wonderful tobacco you must be smoking!' I have even gone through Customs (but not in England) on fragrance alone – when in fact there was nothing re-markable about the tobacco itself: it was being treated properly.

If I were a youth today perhaps I would never start smoking, if only to thumb my nose at these appalling prices. But after fifty years of it, I regret nothing. Man, the creature who knows he must die, who has dreams larger than his destiny, who is for ever working a confidence trick on himself, needs an ally. (Woman I include here in Man.) Mine has been tobacco. Even with it I have too often been impatient and intolerant. Without it I should have been insufferable. You may retort that I am insufferable anyhow, but with a pipe nicely going, I do not believe you.

– Giving Up Conferences –

1966

F or all I know other people may turn down more invitations to conferences than I do. However, their percentage of refusals cannot be higher during these past few years because mine is one hundred per cent. Down they are turned, these invitations, one after another, *flat*.

Not that I am rude about them. I always offer an excuse. I am not very well, I have other long-standing engagements, I am wrestling with some great opus. I bring in a lot of reluctance, am filled with regret. But I make it quite plain that I am not going. And here I be-have better than some of my distinguished colleagues, who accept such invitations, allow their names to go into print, and then never turn up. This is bad. I am ashamed of such distinguished colleagues and some-times doubt (*a*) if they are all that distinguished and (*b*) if they really are colleagues.

But before I explain why I do not attend them, let us be clear about conferences. They are apparently on a high, wide and handsome level. I am not concerned here with a week-end in Wolverhampton in August or three nights at Worthing in February, with delegates arriving by bus and being sent to a Youth Hostel or the

Gladstone Temperance Hotel. Any man over thirty and in his right mind will refuse that sort of invitation.

Most of these conferences I turn down are international, and fares will be paid to Switzerland, Italy, the Island of Rhodes. Rooms have been booked at the Bristol or the Grand. There may be sight-seeing tours laid on, to say nothing of official luncheons and cocktail parties and seats at the opera. They look like Continental holidays for nothing. Why should a man boast (it is a weakness of mine) of turning them down? Is he trying to suggest that he is *so grand* that he can afford to refuse − and even sneer − at such magnificent invitations?

No, madam. (For it is about thirty to one that the last query was feminine.) It is the old hand in me that writes the refusals. I have had my share of these doings. And now I know − and it is high time I did − the limitations of my own temperament and tolerance. Lady, I know what it will be like, and probably you don't. Just listen now.

In the ten years following the War, when public spirit still moved in me, I attended a number of international conferences. On several occasions I was actually the chairman. This is, I must admit, not as bad as it sounds. In fact I would rather 'chair' a conference than simply attend one as a delegate. My method as a chairman was to make a speech, brief but rousing, at the opening session, make another, just as brief, at the closing session, and during the three days in between do nothing official and boring at all, having divided the work among all the other people, who would be toiling over resolutions and amendments and final reports while I was sitting at ease in the nearest bar. But with whom, you may ask. The answer is – with a few rebellious and choice souls who had marched out of their subcommittees or working parties. And sometimes that is how the real work of the conference was done, well away from the conscientious gasbags.

My first complaint against international conferences is that there are so many foreigners attending them. I have a great store of international goodwill except when I am surrounded by foreign delegates, who suddenly seem altogether *too foreign*, as if they were playing irritating character parts. Some I don't mind – usually, the Scandinavian, the Dutch, the Swiss, the Austrian. The worst of the Europeans – and I say this with regret, being a greedy man and fond of France – are the French. M. Toulemonde and his delegation from Paris are conference-wreckers to a man. (They never used to send any women in my time.)

To begin with, they always pretended not to understand a word of English, fighting a rear-guard action for their own language. On being introduced to them, you would mutter a few words of your own miserable French, and then later they would corner you and pour out floods of rapid and idiomatic French, which you nodded and muttered at, hoping they were complaining about the Grand or Bristol Hotel food.

Afterwards, to your horror, you would discover, at some plenary session, that you had apparently already given your support to some monstrous proposal of theirs. Their other trick was to arrive late, in a body, at some meeting, insist upon discussing something not on the agenda, and then depart furiously in a body if they were called to order. No wonder they have to have a de Gaulle.

Delegates from much further afield usually belonged to one of two groups. Either they spoke little but when they did speak could not be understood at all, or they were orators and went on and on and on. Many South Americans, in my conference time, were capable of wasting hours and hours, chiefly for the benefit of the reporter from the *Uruguay Gazette* they had persuaded to attend the session. In Paris once, as chairman, I was challenged to a duel by one such orator, whom I had accused of wasting our time. And if this seems a bit much, I must add that once as chairman in the Central Hall, Westminster, I had fireworks thrown at me, even though I was not rebuking anybody.

Even apart from the boredom of most of the procedure, I have never been able to escape feeling a fool at most of these conferences. There is, I think, something silly about us, the way in which we all arrive together, hand in our names (though I have never yet worn one of those badges they give out) and queue up for programmes, tickets, labels, time-tables, city plans and guides, like sheep who have suddenly developed a taste for print. I may have been too self-conscious and oversensitive, but I always felt that the other people in the hotels and the local citizenry regarded us as so many self-important asses. Moreover, I always had a suspicion that the hotels and restaurants, the ones in which we dined en masse, had earlier been beaten down to their lowest possible prices, so that we figured in their eyes as a miserable lot of cut-rate guests who did not deserve much attention.

And the receptions by the Minister, the Burgo-master, and the rest, did nothing to restore my self-esteem. I felt that in their eyes we were just part of yet another official chore. 'What have I to do tonight?' they probably asked. 'Oh – those fellows. No way of getting out of it, I suppose?' If they hadn't said anything like that, they always seemed to me to look as if they had. After all, who in his senses wants to Welcome a Conference? What is there to say that would not be better left unsaid? What sane man (I am not sure about women) enjoys routine official hospitality?

Not I, for one. Coming close to my idea of Hell is the official diplomatic life, with its endless luncheons, cocktail parties, dinners, receptions, suppers, all packed with the same people saying nothing in particular. It is boring to receive such hospitality, and it must be still more boring to give it. You cannot even drink yourself out of tedium, because either the booze is not strong enough (that thin white wine that does not seem to come from anywhere) or, if potent, then there is not enough of it. And when there are a hundred or so of you – and there can easily be far more in a big conference – all wearing badges and fixed grins, then everything is much worse. The tipple may easily be one part of cheap Barsac and one part of Riesling to four parts water. The only conference guest who has a chance is the chairman, who, if he knows what's what, may escape to a back room and whisky.

Then there is that *Morning* or *Afternoon Sight-seeing*, with which the trap is so often baited. Anything is probably better than listening to men droning on and on in a stuffy room, until you have covered your agenda with doodles, but I am not one who enjoys an official tour of the city and its environs accompanied by special guides who let you off nothing. 'This book,' said the little girl when returning it to her teacher, 'tells me more about penguins than I want to know.' And guides are like that. I took to painting partly in order to avoid sight-seeing when on holiday. And this was private and conjugal sight-seeing, whereas on conferences there may be three or four coach loads of you, yawning and yawning or wondering what could have been wrong with the *fruits-de-mer* served at the cut-rate lunch.

As for those free seats at the opera, it depends where you arc. In Vienna – fine! But in Boojum or Snarksy, you may be in for a terrible evening – and five hours of it too. And if the alternative is the Municipal Theatre, it is ten to one they will be doing, specially for you, a very long and quite incomprehensible historical play ending about a quarter to twelve, by which time you would be ready to rat on the conference's chief resolution if anybody offered you cold beer and hot sausages.

Finally, there is too often about the conference's whole proceedings an air of futility. Gasbags, who love these affairs, will have nearly asphyxiated you. Point-of-order sticklers will have infuriated you. Chairmen (not me) will have said nothing in longer and more pompous terms than you have ever known before. Final resolutions, adopted in despair after the last oxygen has left the room, will seem quite meaningless. And − but here I exclude scientific and technological conferences − instead of feeling more optimistic about international co-operation, you may now have lost all belief in it.

Certainly, madam, I am exaggerating and I am being unfair and it can't be as bad as I say it is. The fact remains though, I turn the invitations down *flat*, even though they come from Venice, Ascona, Dubrovnik, Stockholm. I'm not going. I've given it up.

– Critique of 1972 –

W e are now living in a society that appears – outside its propaganda and advertising – to dislike itself just as much as I dislike it. We are houseguests of the Sorcerer's Apprentice, who has let loose what he can't begin to control. What was not quite so bad yesterday will be much worse tomorrow. The past (we assume) has gone. The present is dubious and mainly unrewarding. As for the future – well, I am now an old hand at this and could be eloquent and fairly terrifying on the nightmare agenda of the world population, global pollution, vanishing natural resources, radioactive garbage, nuclear doomsday or, failing that, half-starved billions staring at endless vistas of concrete and cement – I could, but why should I? . . .

Even now we have allowed ourselves to build capital cities so monstrously overgrown they are no longer manageable and civilised, wrecking human dignity and decency. Men will now plot, lie, cheat, work like demons, to buy what people used to have for nothing: quiet and a little privacy. The old are suspicious of the young; the young despise the old; and all the persons in between, at any age from thirty to sixty, are mostly busy doing something they don't particularly want to do while wondering if their life has any meaning. The happiest faces are seen in the advertiser's dreamland, inhabited by radiant beings who have just bought something.

In the West we are under the spell of Admass. (I coined this term to describe a system, not the victims of it.) We are supposed to be Consumers, and not much else; surely the lowest view mankind has ever taken of itself. We are televised and advertised out of our senses. We exist among images, not realities. And hardly anybody seems to notice that quality is disappearing, chiefly because so many small firms, which took a pride in what they were making and selling, have been taken over by large firms, which take pride only in their dividends.

While money is more and more important, what it buys is steadily getting worse. The 'Good Life' is mostly a swindle; it should be given a bouquet – or better, a wreath – of plastic flowers. In our society everybody envies the very rich – except the people who have met them. Probably for nine-tenths of our younger people their Jerusalem or Mecca, Avalon or Garden of Hesperides, is Las Vegas, one of the stupidest, ugliest, nastiest cities on earth. We have created a society whose representative figures are politicians sold like soap flakes, and men who ask questions on television, and singers who have no voices but only a lot of hair, sweat and electronic equipment, and photographers and models. We are the supreme clever-silly people of man's history.

– On Old Age –

1977

W hy not a section, as honest as I can make it,
on Old Age? A lot of people have told us how
they are enjoying – or have enjoyed their old age. I am
not one of these complacent ancients. I detest being
old. I can't settle down to make the most of it – whatever that may be – but resent almost every aspect of it.
There is still in me a younger man, trapped, struggling
to get out. It is rather as if I were press-ganged at a
stage door, dragged in to submit to *old-man make-up*,
and then pushed on the stage to play an objectionable
character part. For instance, I am increasingly fussy
about engagements and arrangements and time-tables.
Meanwhile, there is a self that is aware of all this fussi-
ness and deplores it. This confirms my opinion that
in old age we are compelled to play a bad character
part, not belonging to our essential and enduring self.
We are out there, facing an intimate audience, making
fools of ourselves.

Anyhow, I am living at the wrong time. Had I been
born even forty or fifty years earlier, I might have enjoyed going on so long. But now, it seems to me, old
age is a liability without the ghost of an asset. The ripe
experience of us who are old is now not of any value.

It may be we have no wisdom, but then is anybody looking for wisdom? We have no longer anything important to contribute. (But then sometimes I feel that those still in their prime haven't very much, with so many huge problems around and so many inadequate solutions.) There have been civilizations of a sort in which the aged have been expected to climb a mountain and vanish for ever in its mists and snow. Perhaps that mountain is still with us – existing in the inner space of our juniors, hoping to forget us.

Certainly if I played my part properly, I would have it easier. I mean by this a fireside-dressing-gown-dotage existence, behind a huge beard garnished with crumbs and egg. But I don't live that kind of life at all. I keep on writing in the morning and early evening, though finishing sooner than I used to do. I am still involved in various kinds of business, even using the long-distance telephone when I feel I can afford to use it. I am down to breakfast at nine, dressing-gowned though, and then after dictating a few letters (if necessary) I go upstairs to shave and dress, usually about 10.30. I come down and work until about 12.50. Unless it is raining I take a short walk in the afternoon, rarely seeing other walkers, only cars, and then I read or do a little work until tea. I am at work again, roughly between 5.30 and 6.30 – only an hour but an hour of actual writing, and not thinking about writing. (I do that at teatime.) Then I go up for a leisurely shower and a change of clothes, not anything much nattier but just a change. Bed about 11.30. Read until about one o'clock, sometimes later. Unless we have house guests, Saturday's programme is much the same. But I am leaving out the social side, dining out or having people in to dine.

But I have a point to make about all this carry-on. Because I am old, almost everything mentioned above demands both effort and patience. Nothing runs itself. What – even getting dressed or going to bed? Certainly. They are both workouts. I don't say tremendous efforts are involved, but there are no easy routines here, nothing accomplished while thinking about something else. I can have a little wrestling match just getting into a pair of trousers. Just coping with the mere arrangements of ordinary living, there must continually be an exercise of will. To get by from 9 in the morning until midnight I use enough willpower to command an army corps. Is there no fun along the way? Yes, of course; but I wish there was more – and much less effort. Any serene old age is still well out of sight. I am in a fair way to become one of the really grumpy old meanies, cackling at the deaths of acquaintances. But of course not of friends.

Here the loss is hideous, really hard to bear. We begin to outlive friendship on a desolating scale. I take one example. Just over fifty years ago, a large group of us, including some famous literary figures, used to meet in a Fleet Street pub to drink and air our wit. Only two of us are left, the other survivor being J. B.

Morton, that glorious wild humorist, *Beachcomber*; and we have lately exchanged letters, and it has been like two small ships flashing signals across a huge darkness. Whatever other people may say, to me it is no joke growing old. Not only do friends vanish, leaving blank spaces, but sometimes the news can be terrible: two of the closest friends I ever had, man and wife, both died horrible lingering deaths. It is true that in the end you grow a kind of carapace, to protect what store of feeling you have left, so that I turn a lacklustre eye on those official appeals for help that come, sometimes quite alone, through the letterbox. I am not yet a very mean old man, but I am moving in that direction. I view with increasing distaste those guests who can leave an inch or so of good wine in their glasses.

A familiar figure, if only in legend, is the old man who sits by the fire, hour after hour, recalling past triumphs. I never find myself doing this, and I suppose I have had my share of triumphs on a writer's modest scale. I am more apt to poke around in my recollections and then discover the mistakes I have made. Here is one of the greatest, a warning perhaps to other but younger writers. It is this. I have spent too much time doing what came naturally to me – writing – when I ought to have turned aside from it far more often to do other things. I could have been digging and planting in the garden. I ought to have started painting much earlier, not leaving it until my sixties. I could have followed Jacquetta's example, enjoying natural history and being knowledgeable about it: my ignorance is appalling. Instead of leaving the piano alone, except for some very rare strumming, I might at least have kept my fingers in practice. Astronomical discoveries and speculations fascinate me – think of those *black holes*! – but I have made no serious study of the science. Indeed, I haven't made a serious study of any subject removed from literature and history. When I was much younger I read a lot of philosophy, but as soon as the linguistic fellows arrived, they turned me off, and I have stayed off ever since. This is a disgraceful record, and if I am now a dissatisfied grumpy old man, it serves me right.

One thing has happened. I have lived long enough now to understand why some people disliked or despised me. And this is new. I am not going so far as to say I ought to have been disliked or despised. What I am saying is that understanding has now replaced furious resentment and indignation. Those people, I see, had some justification. I catch a glimpse of their point of view. But why this change? I think it is because now I am no longer in love with myself, as I must have been once. I may still have a fairly good opinion of myself, as indeed I think we all ought to have. (The mind of any man who really hates or despises himself is a disaster area, always bringing bad news.) But the old self-love affair has vanished, and some measure of understanding has taken its place. Now, recalling various past episodes, I tell myself I asked for trouble.

But how must I account for certain feelings? Do they belong to insight or are they lumps of octogenarian prejudice? Let me take one example. I can't help feeling – even while I try to check myself – that there is now in our world a marked absence of great sure talent. Tremendous ability, in all departments, is hard to find. We look for giant figures, but where are they? (I agree they may be hidden among the labs and behind the paraphernalia of the sciences, just waiting to announce some astounding conclusions.) It is as if we had now created an atmosphere – compounded out of pollution, stress, too many people – in which gigantic personages can't find sufficient nourishment. We are in the dwarf, zombie, robot, business. And even if we are not, we are certainly crowding ourselves out, possibly with not enough space for high excellence to lift its head. This reminds me of an idea that occasionally disturbs me. Suppose there is only so much genius, great talent, high excellence, to go round, so that the more and more people there are at a given time, the poorer and thinner the distribution is, with never a ration to nourish a giant. Thus in the year 2000 anything but the dreariest mediocrity might be unthinkable. Already our political ideologists, bent on rejecting quality in education, are pushing us in that direction.

If all this seems rather harsh, it comes from some bitter reflections. I have suggested already that this is a bad time for any approach to or arrival at old age. We are well out of fashion. But that isn't all, not by a long nasty piece of chalk. Just suppose, reader, you are in your eighties and a grandfather with a large family. You are no treat to look at or to listen to; play no games, no longer drive a car, can't venture on long walks; really a poor old thing. But at any other time but this snarling brute of a time, you could at least *be generous.* That is your role – good old lavish grandpa! To play the role you must be on the spot – and not in some remote taxhaven – and if you are on the spot nowadays, then you can't sustain the role. Most of your money is ruthlessly removed from you – we are in Britain of course – because you are under a government that is only generous, extravagant, carefree about money, to and with and for *itself.* Its attitude towards you is that of a mangle towards damp clothes. Most of what you earn belongs to it, even if necessary before you know what you have been earning. Before you can work out what to give your grandchildren for Christmas, a host of people are on your back, with their hands reaching down to your pockets, removing money that might as well be flung out of the window.

Bitter – eh? Certainly I am bitter, if only because I am old and *I have had enough of it.* I have paid my whack, and now we who are really old – all of us frustrated grandfathers – should at last be *let off* and not badgered, bullied and mulcted right to the edge of the grave. Some years ago, I called at No. 11 Downing Street to appeal to a former Chancellor of the Exchequer. I suggested to him that any man over seventy-five should pay no income tax at all *on earned income.* This would cost the government very little, and would make life much easier for a number of old people, some of them of considerable distinction and still earning their living. (A few jobbing gardeners possibly, but probably far more artists and scientists.) We had a drink and he listened to me attentively. Finally he said he agreed with me in principle, but the reform would be difficult to administrate, if only because all Civil Service pensions were treated as *earned income.* (Collapse of stout party!) These same pensions, I believe, are now to be protected against any erosion by inflation. Nobody can say our government doesn't look after itself and its own. Some of us would like to catch a glimpse of the State wearing the same smiling face. We are of course mostly old and short of temper.

At all times, I seem to remember, I have never played the part a good social life-style has expected me to play. This is certainly true now, when I ought to be a serene and sweet old man, preferably with plenty of snow-white hair and a beautiful beard, not half-bald, clean-shaven and with horrid bags under the eyes. It is, I repeat, the fault of that younger man, trapped by the ruthless years, and still trying to get out. He must be responsible for a snarling graceless old age. And now I have just remembered something I wrote in *Margin Released* about fifteen years ago. Here it is:

. . . Sometimes I wonder if I was unlucky in my birthplace.

Further south I might now be called *maître* and, wearing a skullcap, receive homage every Thursday night and Sunday afternoon. Further north and east, clear-eyed solemn maidens might bring flowers to the house on my birthday. Unfortunately we have no sensible English equivalent of these signs of public esteem, except those pats on the head and shoulder from the Establishment, meant for better or worse men, not for me . . .

But now let us be clear about all this. I would be embarrassed by gatherings of admirers or maidens bringing flowers, and have firmly declared my lack of interest in Establishment honours, traditionally unwelcome in my profession. All I ask in fact is to be let alone, to cope as best I can – and in private – with the weaknesses, the constant demands on willpower, of old age. But, in a bad sense, I am not left to myself. As I have already declared, I am increasingly badgered, bullied and mulcted. I am recognized officially only as a pip that must be made to squeak, so that the state can make more and more daft investments. I am not an aged man who has done some service but a milch cow. And so, though no disciple of Dylan Thomas, I refuse to go gentle into that good night. You might say I alternate between a general grumpiness and downright anger. And clearly there are better ways of spending one's final years.

However, there is something else, much more impersonal, that ought to be said. A State that taxes ferociously while spending freely itself is a danger. It wears two very different masks: one is Dick Turpin, the other is Santa Claus. Wearing Turpin it confiscates so much that a man may earn a good income and yet have little opportunity to be charitable himself, as he could be forty years ago. As Santa Claus, spending money it has never earned itself but only grabbed, it may be regarded by millions as the fount from which all blessings flow. Increasingly it becomes more and more powerful, a threat to the ancient liberties of its subjects. The sheer size and weight of its bureaucratic machinery become daunting. Moreover, what it does tends to be expensive, clumsy, ungracious. Even when I was a socialist I was never a State socialist believing – rather vaguely, I must confess – in a common ownership belonging to cooperatives, public corporations, and the like. The State, in my book, was always a big clumsy bully. To allow it to confiscate more and more, to spend more and more on itself, to acquire more and more power, seemed to me even then a disaster. And this I feel even more strongly now, when any chances I may have to be compassionate and generous are rapidly dwindling, when harder work only attracts larger and more ruthless demands, when the very idea of a *windfall*, once such a treat in my profession, can now be dismissed. And if, on top of all this, the very notion of a liberal freedom-loving democracy is shrinking and in peril, then I can hardly be blamed if I alternate, as I have already declared, between a general grumpiness and downright anger. It is well beyond a joke to live so long, only to become the victim of fanatical ideologists, the very people I have always detested. Certainly I could think of far better ways of spending my final years.

– About Hating Airports –

1977

S ome people will say at once that I hate airports
because in secret I dread flying. And they will be
quite wrong. I have been flying all over and round the
world for many years. I have had some bad flights of
course but they have never deterred me from going
off again. True, on flights of any length I have always
travelled first class. This is not for social grandeur,
smoked salmon and champagne (I don't even enjoy it),
but because I am a bulky man and the space allotted
to tourist passengers becomes unendurable after a few
hours. I must also admit that I am not happy in those
tiny light planes that seem to be concocted out of three
deck chairs and a propeller. Nor is that all. I don't in
fact hate small airports, in which I have landed and
taken off all over the place. It is large airports, like
Heathrow or Kennedy, that depress me so that I begin
to hate them.

It may seem odd, at least at a first glance, that I
also said I could often enjoy railway stations. There is
nothing personal about travelling by train. (It was different once in America, where you did some personal
booking and then, while on the train, appeared to be
continually visited by two oldish men, who always

wore rimless spectacles and looked exactly alike.) You
buy a ticket at the station; a man looks at it when you
go on to the platform; you board the train; nothing
could be more impersonal. (You might be a madman
and nobody would know.) On the other hand, in the
airport, you have a name as well as a ticket, and if you
are late getting on to the plane your name is called out
over the public address system: they are actually looking for you, whereas nobody in a railway station cares
if you never board the train. So how can I say that I
enjoy one and detest the other?

To answer that we must briefly return to the Essay
text. There I described myself as a nervous apprehensive traveller. I didn't mean that I am in a fearful
state about the journey itself. Not at all. The truth is,
I am always nervous and apprehensive about *missing*
the plane or train, so that I always insist upon arriving
early, dreading any last-minute rush. (Moreover, years
ago, I missed the Barcelona-Paris Express, and con-
demned myself to catching local trains all over France,
paying more and more, first for frustration and then
for increasing boredom. A lesson, I can tell you!) So, as
I like to arrive early, I am referring to railway stations
and large airports in terms of waiting in them. The
official procedure may be more impersonal in stations,
but the places themselves seem to be far closer to ordinary warm human living. They exist, in a far better atmosphere. The large airports will give you a name, and
will cry or boom it out if you have not arrived in the

plane; but even so they exist in an atmosphere withering to true personality, an atmosphere in which you are no longer a fellow human being, *a man and a brother.*

So I feel, as I wait, that a huge machine, some triumph of technology, has taken over. It is quite a polite and even considerate machine, aware of your name and wanting you to start your journey. But this is so that a list can be properly checked. The complicated machine has to function properly. You now exist, as you wait, in a conditioned air that begins to be diminishing and desiccating. You are less than half your usual self, and the people all round you in the great lounge hall look at least as bad as you feel, many of them so drooping and mournful. Even the brassy drinking type – another for the road, old boy – are clearly overdoing character parts. Even if there is music, it is machine music, provided by some distant orchestra of robots. The monstrously amplified announcements – *Ruritania Airways announce the departure, etc.* – never varying in tone, offer us no breath of life, no hint of fellow-feeling. The machine has spoken. The uniformed girls; trim and smiling, who conduct us here and there, seem far removed from the delicious wayward creatures their boy-friends know as girls. The bus to the plane or that walk across the tarmac are not warmed by any laughter or even smiles. We might be on our way to some kind of concentration camp. We are in the grip of the machine.

We can give a guess at the way the world has been

going if we consider transport down the years. Notice its send-off. If the old prints are to be believed – and I think they are – the stagecoaches left their inns with trumpets, bugles, horns sounding, all manner of blown kisses and wavings, inn loungers cheering and urchins turning somersaults. The journey itself might be uncomfortable but it always started in fine style. The same might be said of most ships, moving off after a wealth of incidents, last drinks, fond farewells, cheers galore and perhaps a band playing. (I often departed in ships during the '20s and '30s, when I could still afford to pay the passages. The best send-off of all was when I sailed from San Francisco to Tahiti in 1931 – such a rich warm scene, so many songs, flowers, smiles and tears, shoutings and wavings, with a billowing carpet of petals following us!) Even to board a long-distance train, some noble express, was to take part in an event, with the platform filled with people blowing last kisses and waving us away, as if we were bound on an adventure. And now where have we got to? In airports no last farewells; no flowers, no tears, no smiles. Lost in the machine, glum and silent, we are herded to the tarmac and the most recent example of advanced technology, which will take us to another airport just like the one we left. The lively event, the warmth, the fun, have gone. It is, at heart, a deadly bore.

– On Happiness –

1977

I suspect that my idea of happiness differs from that of most people. It is because of this that I have often been at cross-purposes with them. My happiness is well removed from pleasure. It is not simply enjoyment. Though never slow with a grumble, I have been all my life a great enjoyer, ranging from Beethoven's *Missa Solemnis* to any fine large pork pie with a darkish crust. (And didn't I write a book called *Delight*?) I am no finicky taster of life but have always brought with me a splendid appetite. If praise is deserved at all, I pour it out with never a hint of a growl. For many years I reviewed books of my own choosing; then if I disliked a book, could find nothing good to say of it, I never gave it a notice; I would praise or keep silent. But all this enjoyment, to my mind, has no connection with happiness. Neither has a contented busyness, which many people remember as giving them a happy time. I am not against this judgment, which seems to me reasonable enough, but it is not for me.

My happiness has a special quality, not to be found any morning, evening, lazy afternoon. I am not now mistaking it for ecstasy, much rarer still. But my happiness can't be planned for, arranged, built up. It suddenly arrives out of the blue where it really belongs. There is no *excuse* for it. It is rather as if a fantastic bird had alighted near me and then burst into *song*. Or as if I walked down a familiar road and found myself inside a great blue bubble. Very soon, no doubt, the bird will fly away or the bubble will dissolve into a few scattered drops. I am never given fat helpings of my happiness. I can't call with it at the bank or take it to dine out at a neighbour's. Forty-nine times out of fifty I am alone when it happens, perhaps out walking or having a bath. But suddenly – there it is – and I realize that I am happy. (I agree there can be a retrospective sense of happiness – and some people would argue there is no other kind – but clearly here I am at odds with such people, my experience always being immediate and quite definite.) Such then is my happiness.

Now let us turn over the coin so that its bright face is hidden. The dull side is seen on those occasions when I have been expected to be happy, when people have said, 'You must be feeling very happy.' And there is no sign of this. My face – heavy enough, anyhow – announces that my spirits, if anything, have been drooping. There I am – refusing to feel happy. What is the matter with me? I must be a miserably ungrateful or arrogant fellow, with utterly unreasonable expectations. Who am I – to shrug or scowl when any decent man would be beaming? This is the last time we bother with this chap. Why waste our praises and applause on him? We'll keep them for a more modest friendly man. And that, madam, is how I give myself a bad name.

Yet I am really innocent. Indeed, there is an almost childlike innocence in my idea of happiness, always coming unexpectedly out of the blue. Remember, I make no claim on it. If it descends upon me, well and good and even better. But this *You must be feeling very happy* stuff really belongs to another world, one of accounts, of debits and credits, of getting on in this life, of creeping up to the Top (whatever that is); all a long way from that fantastic bird that suddenly alights and sings, from that blue bubble you enter on a walk or in the bath. And all this is not what is understood by a whole series of bystanders. I have already declared in print that while I have a lot of talent, I have no genius. And I was wrong. I have a genius for being misunderstood. For instance, about happiness.

nh Notting Hill Editions

Notting Hill Editions is devoted to the best in essay writing. Our authors, living and dead, cover a broad range of non-fiction, but all display the virtues of brevity, soul and wit.

Our commitment to reinvigorating the essay as a literary form extends to our website, where we host the wonderful Essay Library, a home for the world's most important and enjoyable essays, including the facility to search, save your favourites and add your comments and suggestions.

To discover more, please visit
www.nottinghilleditions.com

Other titles from Notting Hill Editions*

The Foreigner: Two Essays on Exile
by Richard Sennett

In this pair of essays Sennett visits two of the world's greatest
cities at crucial moments in their history: nineteenth-century
Paris, with its community of political exiles, and the Jewish
Ghetto of Renaissance Venice, where restrictions on outsider
groups had surprising cultural consequences.

Confessions of a Heretic
by Roger Scruton

A collection of provocative essays by the influential social
commentator Roger Scruton. Scruton seeks to answer the
most pressing problems of our age: what can we do to protect
Western values against Islamic extremism? How can we
nurture real friendship in the age of social media? How should
we achieve a timely death against the advances of modern
medicine?

'One of the few intellectually authoritative voices in modern
British conservatism.' – *The Spectator*

My Prizes
by Thomas Bernhard

Bernhard's memoir tells the story of the various farces that
developed around the literary prizes Bernhard received in his
lifetime. His participation in the awards ceremony – always less
than gracious – ended inevitably in scandal.

'Thank goodness for Thomas Bernhard, the most truthful, the
funniest and the most musical of writers since Marcel Proust.'
– Gabriel Josipovici

Portrait Inside My Head
by Phillip Lopate

In this revealing collection of personal essays, renowned
essayist Phillip Lopate shares his unique views on the big
subjects of parenthood, marriage, sex, friendship, and 'the nail
parings of daily life'.

'As riveting as short stories, with arresting openings, sculptured
scenes worthy of fiction . . . and haunting conclusions that
resonate . . . Delightful.' – *The New York Times*

CLASSIC COLLECTION

The Classic Collection brings together the finest essayists of the
past, introduced by contemporary writers.

*Beautiful and Impossible Things
– Selected Essays of Oscar Wilde*
Introduced by Gyles Brandreth

Words of Fire – Selected Essays of Ahad Ha'am
Introduced by Brian Klug

Essays on the Self – Selected Essays of Virginia Woolf
Introduced by Joanna Kavenna

*All That is Worth Remembering
– Selected Essays of William Hazlitt*
Introduced by Duncan Wu

*All NHE titles are available in the UK, and some titles are
available in the rest of the world. For more information, please
visit www.nottinghilleditions.com.

A selection of our titles are distributed in the US and Canada
by New York Review Books. For more information on available
titles, please visit www.nyrb.com.